# OUTLINES
# OF
# HINDU METAPHYSICS

# OUTLINES
## OF
# HINDU METAPHYSICS

MANMATHA NATH SHASTRI, M. A., M. R. A. S.

GYAN

*Published by*

Gyan Publishing House
5, Ansari Road
Daryaganj, New Delhi-110002
Phone: 011-47034999, 9811692060
E-mail: books@gyanbooks.com

*Distribution Network*
gyanbooks.com
India, USA, Canada, UK, Australia, France



ISBN: 978-81-212-8684-8 (PB)
First Published, 1904

2nd Impression 2023

*Printed at:* Gyan Press, Delhi.



**OUTLINES OF HINDU METAPHYSICS**
Author: Manmatha Nath Shastri

# OUTLINES

OF

# HINDU METAPHYSICS.

# OUTLINES

OF

# HINDU METAPHYSICS.

BY

MANMATHA NATH SHASTRI, M.A., M.R.A.S.

*Author of The Buddha,—His Life, Teachings and Order, English Translator of "The Ramayana," "The Mahabharata" &c., &c.*

CALCUTTA:

SOCIETY FOR THE RESUSCITATION OF INDIAN LITERATURE.

40 NAYAN CHAND DUTT'S STREET.

1904.

CALCUTTA, ELYSIUM PRESS,—H. C. DASS, PRINTER,
40, NAYAN CHAND DUTT'S STREET.

To

H. H. MAHARAJA KRISHNA RAJ WOODYAR
BAHADUR OF MYSORE.

THIS WORK

IS RESPECTFULLY DEDICATED

AS A TOKEN OF

SINCERE REGARDS AND HIGH ESTEEM

FOR

HIS HIGHNESS'

CULTURE AND SYMPATHY

WITH ALL GOOD UNDERTAKINGS

BY

HIS HUMBLE AND DEVOTED ADMIRER

The Author.

# PREFACE.

IN presenting the following pages before the public I have but a few words to say. While carrying on my studies in Hindu Philosophy, I felt the want of a handy volume in which a beginner, or one who has not the time and opportunity of going through the numberless volumes in Sanskrit, dealing with this branch of Hindu literature, can find ready at hand a systematic exposition of the various important problems of Hindu Metaphysics. The absence of such a book, I believe, has stood in the way of the popularizing of Hindu Philosophy both in this country and in the West.

It is undoubtedly very difficult for an ordinary student to grasp the true import of the various problems of existence which the Hindu Rishis have sought to solve in many learned treatises for the edification of their succeeding generations, inasmuch as these disquisitions are more or less of an abstrue nature and intended chiefly for advanced students of the Sanskrit language and literature. And then even in Sanskrit there is not a single book in which all important Metaphysical questions have been systematically treated in a regular order and sequence.

To remove this want, which at least I myself felt very much, I have gleaned these sheafs from my own field of labour with a view that they may be of some use to general readers and students of Hindu Philosophy.

I have tried to explain the various important topics relating to Hindu Metaphysics in the light of the elucidation of those subjects by the Rishis. I have also attempted to make the expositions as much popular as I could, avoiding technicalities to the extent which is possible in the treatment of such abstruse topics.

I have spared no pains and trouble to make this little treatise a preparatory ground for the study of higher subjects, and my labours will be amply rewarded if, by the perusal of my humble work, one single reader feels himself interested in the study of Hindu Metaphysics.

ELYSIUM BOWER,
BARAHANAGAR,
AUGUST, 1904.

THE AUTHOR.

# CONTENTS.


| Chapter. | Subject. | Page. |
|---|---|---|
| I. | The Divine Being; His True Nature ... ... ... | 1 |
| II. | Maya ... ... ... | 11 |
| III. | The Theory of Evolution ... | 21 |
| IV. | The Three Gunas or Universal Tendencies of Nature ... | 33 |
| V. | Monism and Dualism ... ... | 79 |
| VI. | Can man know God? ... ... | 87 |
| VII. | God-Vision ... ... | 93 |
| VIII. | Seeking after God ... ... | 97 |
| IX. | The Theory of a Personal God... | 105 |
| X. | Yoga or Communion with God ... | 115 |
| XI. | Mental Discipline ... ... | 151 |
| XII. | Spiritual Discipline ... ... | 163 |
| XIII. | Mukti or Emancipation ... | 187 |
| XIV. | Emancipation in Life ... ... | 195 |
| XV. | The Paths of Emancipation ... | 201 |
| XVI. | The Ideal of True Happiness ... | 225 |
| XVII. | The Necessity of Upasana ... | 235 |

# OUTLINES
OF
# HINDU METAPHYSICS.

## CHAPTER I.

### THE DIVINE BEING: HIS TRUE NATURE.

HINDU RISHIS have always meditated on their *Brahma* or Supreme Deity in His two aspects, namely the *Saguna* or immanent, and the *Nirguna* or transcendent. The entire universe is resolvable into two factors, *viz.*, Nature and God. By the former may be understood the "totality of perceptible phenomena, and by the latter the eternal ground or cause whose essence they express." God is Himself the Real Absolute, and Nature is His objective manifestation. He is the eternal abiding ground, and Nature is the transient phenomenon. God is what *is*, and Nature is what *appears*. Thus in His true and real nature God is transcendent: He is immanent when He manifests Himself in Nature. The relation of God with the objective world is governed by three *Gunas* or qualities. These *Gunas* are the qualities or primary elements which constitute the entire objective world. These three principles are the essential ingredients with which every object of Nature, from a man to an insect, from a mountain to a grass, is formed. These are the three universal tendencies which govern the relation of the universe with God, the relation of the Object with the Subject. These are the forms in which the Absolute Reality manifests Itself. These three *Gunas* are the *Sattwa* or the principle of organisation, the *Rajas* or the principle of self-attraction, and the *Tamas* or the principle of disorganisation. When God manifests Himself in Nature, He appears in these forms, and as such, He is called immanent or *Saguna*. When God is in Nature, when the objective world is viewed in its relarion to, and dependence on, its Author, He is *Saguna*. Immanency is attributable to God only when He manifests Himself in Nature, only when the relation of the Object with the Subject is taken into consideration. The phenomena of Nature are objects which are not eternal. They are not permanent entities and undergo changes. And so they must be related to an Eternal Subject, an abiding ground that remains unchanged in the midst of changes. No one can help thinking of something behind what he sees or feels. The colour, the form, the sound are not floating attributes,—they are attached undoubtly. to a permanent ground. This Eternal Essence, from which all objects of Nature proceed, this permanent abiding ground, which sends out all phenomena of Nature, this Absolute Reality which suffers no changes, is the *Nirguna Brahma* of the Hindu Rishis. God is transcendent as the Absolute Reality—the Absolute Truth, Intelligence and Bliss—*sat, chit, anandam.* This is the True Nature of God that has been so often described in glowing terms by the Rishis of the Upanishads.

The Sacred Scriptures of the Hindus speak of God as both *Saguna* and *Nirguna*, as manifesting Himself in Nature and again transcending the objects of Nature—as partaking of the qualities or *gunas* of Nature and again transcending them. In the *Isá Upanishad* it is said :—

" It (Brahma) moves, but (truly) does not move : it is near, it is also distant. It is inside all this, and outside all this."*

---

* तदेजति तन्नैजति तद्दूरे तद्वन्तिके ।
तदन्तरस्य सर्व्वस्य तदु सर्व्वस्यास्य बाह्यतः ॥

*Vide* Verse V.

It is again said in the *Katha Upanishad*:

"The Being of Whom all the Vedas sing, for Whom all penances are done, for attaining Whom men perform Brahmacharyya, that Being is, in short, indicated by the syllable OM."

"This Indestructible is *Brahma*, this Indestructible is *Para-Brahma*. Whoever wishes for a thing in view of this Indestructible, gets it."*

Similarly many other S'ruti texts clearly prove that the Rishis of the Upanishads contemplated the Divine Being both as *Saguna* and *Nirguna*. The former aspect

---

* सर्व्वे वेदा यत्पदमामनन्ति
तपांसि सर्वाणि च यद्वदन्ति ॥
यदिच्छन्तो ब्रह्मचर्य्यञ्चरन्ति
तत्ते पदं संग्रहेण ब्रवीम्योमित्येतम् ।
एतद्ध्येवाक्षरं ब्रह्म एतद्ध्येवाक्षरम्परम् ।
एतद्ध्येवाक्षरं ज्ञात्वा यो यदिच्छति तस्य तत् ॥

*Vide* Chap. I, Valli II, Verse 15—16.

of the Divine Nature is transitory, subject to change, relative and dependent, while the latter is essential, absolute and eternal. The *Saguna* aspect is limited in time and space, while the *Nirguna* transcends all such limitations. The *Saguna* is ever-changing and whirling, the *Nirguna* is enduring, central, regulative, and reposing eternally in the midst of changes. The *Saguna* is accidental, while the *Nirguna* is essential. The *Saguna* aspect is finite, the *Nirguna* is infinite. The *Saguna* excludes the *Nirguna*, but the *Nirguna* comprehends the *Saguna*. The finite cannot contain the infinite, but the infinite can comprehend the finite.

It is for this reason that the Rishis of the Upanishads hold that the *Nirguna* describes the nature of God in its absolute truth. Thus the conception of the *Nirguna* is the conception of the True and Absolute Divine Being. The true nature of God, according to the Rishis, is *Nirguna*. It is only when His powers are alluded to in His manifestation in the objects of Nature that He is called *Saguna*. They have therefore given a decided preference to the worship of the *Nirguna*, though oftentimes their disciples are exhorted to contemplate the *Saguna* aspect of the Divine Being. It is, indeed, very difficult to conceive One, Absolute, Infinite Being—but it is not so very difficult to conceive Him in Nature, to contemplate Him as the Author of the objective world and exercising His power in its preservation and destruction. The latter, though practically infinite, is, really speaking, relative and finite. The *Nirguna* indicates the true nature of the Divine Being, while the *Saguna* describes His power, which though infinite in nature, depends upon time and space for its manifestation. From the contemplation of the *Saguna* aspect of God one can arrive at that of the *Nirguna*—which is the ultimate goal of the spiritual exercises of a worshipper. The *Nirguna* or absolute attributes of God include the *Saguna* or relative attributes. The only difference between them is that the former describes the true Nature of the Divine Being, and the latter how He manifests Himself in Nature and governs the creation. Though the first stage in a man's religious culture is the contemplation of the *Saguna* aspect, the ultimate goal, however, is that of the *Nirguna.*

The *Kena* S'ruti thus describes Him:—

"He is the ear of the ear, the mind of the mind, the speech of the speech, the *prána* of the *prána*, and the eye of the eye.

"He is not to be seen by the eyes, not to be described by words, not to be conceived by the mind. We do not know Him. Know Him as *Brahma* Who is indescribable in words, but Who (*i.e.*, Whose power) gives utterance to words.

"People cannot conceive Him in their mind, but He knows it. Know Him as *Brahma.*

"Know Him as *Brahma* Whom people cannot see with their eyes, but through Whose power they see all objects of vision."*

* श्रोत्रस्य श्रोतं मनसो मनो यद्वाचोऽवाचं च उ प्राणस्य प्राणश्चक्षुषश्चक्षुः।

न तत्र चक्षुर्गच्छति न वाग गच्छति नो मनो॥

*Vide* Verse 2—3.

## CHAPTER II.

### MAYA.*

"FOR a right interpretation of the broad outlines of the Vedanta Philosophy one must begin with Māyā. It is a term pretty commonly used, but with wide distinctions. It has a scientific, and a popular, signification, both of which it will be our purpose to shew in the present notice.

"'Māyā has been defined as the inherent force residing in the Supreme *Brahma*,—which is essentially existent and which cannot be differentiated. As the consuming flame of fire imparts an idea of its force, so

* We glean this from a valuable contribution by Dr. NANDALAL DHOLE, the eminent translator of the *Panchadasi* in the columns of *The Philosophic Inquirer*, Vol. VII, p. 73, and insert it here with the kind permission of his son, our esteemed friend and brother BABU HEERALAL DHOLE.

the potentiality of force, present in Self, is plainly seen in the objective world. But this Māyā cannot be said to be one with *Para-Brahma*, nor as something distinct, in the same way as the consuming force of a fire cannot be said to be the fire itself. Then, if again, you admit it as a separate entity, you cannot by any means describe its separate existence.'

"It will thus be evident that Māyā and *Para-Brahma* are but different names for Matter and Force. We all know force cannot exist without Matter as a separate entity, yet to say that it is the same as matter, is absurd. Hence in the text quoted,* we find the non-dualist asking his opponent, a Madhyamika Buddhist, to describe force as a separate entity. But it may be urged that *Para-Brahma* is force, and we have seen Māyā to be also a force—therefore we have force + force—or force within force—something equally absurd,

* *Panchadasi*, Book II, Verse 42—43.

a condition which the mind fails to comprehend. But such apparent ambiguity is far from real. For Māyā is matter in its undifferentiated condition,—a condition in which the difference between matter and its indwelling potentiality is minimised to the lowest numerical figure; it is the boundary line of Matter and Force,—where Matter, losing its grossness, assumes the subtlety of *super-ethereal finis*, where no Matter is distinguishable as such, but all is Spirit or Force. And such an inference is drawn from Nature. To quote a familiar illustration, the transition from a mineral to a vegetable and from a vegetable to an animal is so gradual, that it is impossible to distinguish the one from the other. Even at the present moment, science is undecided as to whether certain classes of the lowest vegetables belong to the mineral class, or the last in the scale of the animal series belongs to the vegetable. So much do they resemble each other. If such a view be accepted, the apparent inconsistency is removed. Virtually, then, the difference between *Mula-Prakriti* (Matter in its undifferentiated cosmic condition) and *Purusha* (its spirit or *Para-Brahma*) for all practical purposes is nil. Hence the Western Materialist, denying Spirit all over, concentrates his attention on his material atoms, which, with their indwelling potentiality, supply him with a sufficient cause to answer for every phenomenon. The Vedantist, therefore, presents the sharp point of a double-edged sword to his opponent, which takes the ground from under his feet and makes his own position invincible.

Now Māyā is described as a Force and it is elsewhere defined as something indescribable, which is neither existence *(sat)* nor non-existence *(asat)*—in short it is one with Ignorance, which, again, being the chief factor of the grand Cosmos, is the same as the Prakriti of Kapila. Therefore Māyā is nothing less than matter. Now this Māyā existed potentially in *Para-Brahma*, and if we say, that by an act of volition He created the objective world from the very same Māyā, we imply no such contradiction as the Hebrew account of God's creating the world out of nothing. But, then, we may be asked, *Para-Brahma* is an impersonality, and volition is due to consciousness, which It can lay no claims to. To such of our task-masters, we reply that matter *per se* is unconscious and inert, and can bring forth nothing until acted upon by an intelligent Force and that *Para-Brahma* is Consciousness itself; consequently the impress of change which It produces in the mass of inert matter to make it evolve things varied and innumerable, is tantamount to the volitional agency of a Personal Creator. Then, again, if it be asked, since *Para-Brahma* is a pure Spirit, how can It have any connection with Matter, which is Its antagonist?—Our reply is that Spirit and Force are, as we have seen, convertible terms, and we have likewise seen that Force cannot exist without Matter, hence wherever there is Force there Matter must always be. To sum up, then, we find that Māyā existed in *Para-Brahma*, and it is the same Māyā which brought forth the universe in a natural order of sequence by undergoing mutations impressed upon it through its force or *Para-Brahma*. It is unnecessary here to dwell upon the consecutive series of changes; suffice it to say that from its undifferentiated condition,—a state in which it had no properties to distinguish it, for properties are due to the elements, ether and the rest,—its pre-elementary condition, if we may be allowed such an expression, it became subtle, and then gross, and ultimately quintuplicated. Change, then, is the law of the universe; without it the world would lose its freshness and beauty; change everywhere and at every moment is the grand centric law round which are deposited the nuclei of future planets, their satellites, etc., as it surely leads to the slow and gradual but sure disintegration of the existing ones. In this way there never was a time when the world was non-existent, nor will there ever be a time when it will be totally destroyed (Kapila); though in truth it may be laid down that the earth we inhabit is not the first of the series and that our human race is not the first that has been called into existence. From close reasoning this must naturally establish itself. For if *Para-Brahma* is eternal and essentially existent, and if such a *Para-Brahma* must have its Māyā wherein to reside, if the contact of the two induces changes which are usually called creative, but are, strictly speaking, evolutional, then where is the beginning and the end in such a plan?

Another signification of Māyā is *Illusion*. This consists in believing the world and all its goods to be real, and thus being enticed to hunger after material comforts. As an apt illustration we may refer to the story of Nārada. Nārada was enquiring of Krishna one day what Māyā was. They were travelling together in a sandy waste; Nārada felt thirsty, and wanted some water to drink; a shed was pointed out, where he repaired, leaving his companion to wait for him. The proprietress of the shed happened to be a young damsel whom Nārada had no sooner seen, than he fell head and ears over in love. His thirst for drink was gone, but he was now possessed with a thirst for obtaining the fair creature's hands. He marries her, he gets several children and removes with his family from place to place to avoid disasters till ultimately his wife and family are drowned while crossing the bed of a river; and he is found bewailing the loss of his dearly beloved wife. In such a juncture Hari puts in appearance. To his queries Nārada gives no reply, but intent on grief he weeps as loudly as ever. He is fully ensnared into the meshes of Māyā. Bhagavan deprives him of the charm, when lo! Nārada is again restored to *jnâna*. He had seen Māyā."

## CHAPTER III.

### THE THEORY OF EVOLUTION.

BRAHMA is the one Reality without a second that underlies. the many. It is the impersonal Absolute Self. It is *Sachchidánanda*, "existent, intelligence and beatitude." It is called *Sat* or existent, because it is the source of existence or manifestation to all that is known and seems to be. It is called *chit* or intelligence, because it imparts light to all things. It is called *ánanda* or beatitude, because it is free from the miseries of repeated births, from every sort of pain and sorrow. Brahma is also called *nityashuddhabuddhamukta* or ever pure, intelligent and free. It is ever pure, because no sort of impurity exists in Brahma. It is free from desire, aversion, passion and illusory limitations or *upadhi*. It is intelligent, because it lights up or manifests all individual spirits. It illumines the unconscious modifications of the sensory. It is free, because it is not implicated in *avidyá* or unreality and therefore it neither acts nor suffers from the effects of *Karma*. According to the Vedantist Brahma *is* and everything else *seems to be*,—*i.e.*, Brahma alone is real and everything else is unreal.

Brahma is both the *upádána* and the *nimitta*, *i.e.*, the material and operative cause of the world. It is the material cause, for the entire universe is merely the outward manifestation of *Brahma Sattwa* or the divine existence. The *Samsára* or the transmigatory series fictitiously overlies it. Brahma is called the operative cause, because Prakriti, or the world-projecting illusion, which is inert or inactive by nature, becomes active when it comes into contact with Brahma. Iron is by nature inert, but it is set to motion by a loadstone. Such is the case with Prakriti and Brahma.

The evolution of the universe or the work of creation begins when *Prakriti* or Māyā comes into contact with or into proximity to Brahma. Evolution, in Vedantic parlance, is called *Nâmarupavyakârana*, or "differentiation under name and form." As plants originate from seeds and seeds from plants, so the processes of evolution and dissolution follow one another from eternity to eternity. "There never was a time when there was no creation. Creation and Creator are two lines without beginning and without end, running parallel to each other. God is powerful and ever-active Providence, under whose power systems after systems are being evolved out of chaos, made to run after for a time and again destroyed. This is what the Hindu boy repeats every day with his Guru 'The sun and the moon the Lord created after other suns and moons'." The world is a series, beginningless and endless, of bodies and environments through which individual souls, that is the one soul regarding itself as many under the influence of *Máyá* or illusion, pass. They pass through it for the fruition of work or *bhoga*. Thus embodiments proceed from works and works again proceed from embodiments.

The process of evolution is thus described by the Vedanta philosophers :—

(1) When Brahma is overspread with Māyā or illusion it manifests itself as Içwara. The illusion of Içwara is identical with that of each and every *Jiva* or sentiency. This illusion is at once one and many. As one, it is the *Kárana Sharira,* or casual body of Içwara; and as many, it is the *ánandamaya-kosha,* or the beatific involucrum of the *Jivas.* Içwara and Jiva are essentially identical. In the order of evolution they are in a state of *Sushupti*, dreamless sleep or beatitude. That state is called *Sushupti* in which *Jiva* or the individual soul longs for no object and sees no dream. In this state Brahma manifests itself

as Içwara or Demiurgus in whom, the illusory universe, viewed separately in the dreaming state of sleep (*svapna*) and of waking (*jágrat*) exists as one and in whom is centered the knowledge of all objects, who is bliss and the blissful subject, whose nouth is knowledge and who is endued with *Prajnâ*, discriminating knowledge. Içwara is the lord of all, omniscient, omnipresent, the source of all and the cause of the evolution of all creatures. The work of Içwara is to allot to the transmigrating spirits their several bodies according to *adrista* or the secretly operating law of reward and retribution, and take them back into him at the dissolution of the Kalpa or æon. The Demiurgus does this work by Māyā, the world-projecting illusion or his all-creative power. The great Shankara, in the celebrated commentary of the *Vedanta Sutras*, thus, describes Māyā;—"Name and form, the fictitious products of illusion and the body of the omniscient Demiurgus—name and form, inexplicable as entity and non-entity, the germs of the transmigratory series, are called the illusion, the power, the productiveness of Içwara or the Demiurgus."

(2) United with Prakriti or all-creative power, *Brahma next manifests itself as* Hiranyagarbha. As *one*, *it is* Hiranyagarbha or *Taijasa;* as many it is the *Jivas* or sentiencies in the state of dreaming sleep or *svapna*. In this state imperceptible elements or Tanmātras are evolved. Brahma in this state, *i.e.*, Hiranyagarbha, is cognizant of those objects which are perceptible by the mind. It has no external organs by which it comes into contact with gross objects. Only subtle objects are perceptible to Hiranyagarbha. Out of these subtle elements the vestures of the spirit in its passage from body to body are evolved. The soul, clothed with tenuous involucrum, is called Jivātman or individual soul and passes from one body

to another. The tenuous involucra consist of three sacs, laid one over the other, *viz.*, the cognitional sac, the sensorial sac, and the respiratory sac.

(3) United with Māyā, Brahma next manifests itself as Vaiswānara or Virāt. As one it is Virāt, as many it is *Jivas* in the waking state. Every man, every sentiency, is Brahma illusorily identified with this or that tangible object. The perceptible are evolved out of imperceptible elements in this state. In addition to its own every later element has the properties of the earlier ones. Ether has the property of sound; air, the properties of ether, *i.e.*, tangibility and colour; water, the properties of air, *i.e.*, tangibility, colour, and taste; earth, the properties of air, *i.e.*, tangibility, colour, taste and smell. Of these elements are formed the bodies of individual souls which pass from one body to another, as well as their various spheres of fruition. The gross bodies of the *Jivatmas* in

which they move about in this world are made of these gross elements.

Thus according to the Vedanta, the last principle of creation is Brahma, the Supreme Spirit, the Absolute, Impersonal Self, besides whom there is nothing else. It is the First Cause, both of the substance and the form of the world. Compared with him, all other things are not existing and bear predicates opposite to his own. They are, hence, without consciousness and existence in themselves; the existence which they possess is only a derived one and their first and absolute cause is Brahma. The world then, or the thing which does not really exist, and which is without consciousness, is pervaded by Brahma and, hence, ensues the creation or manifestation of the universe, by which the differences which exist already, although in an unmanifested state, become manifest.

The most important difference between the Vedantic theory of evolution and the

Sānkhya is that the former recognises an intelligent Creator as *Içwara*, or Demiurgus while the latter does not. According to the Sānkhya it is the soul and matter from which creation proceeds. Creation depends upon a principle whose nature is activity. This is *Mula-Prakriti*, the first productive nature. It is the material cause from which all effects are produced. The soul, on the contrary, is merely perceiving, witnessing, thinking, without any object that is perceived. According to the Sānkhya there are innumerable souls or spirits. The order of creation or of production, however, is almost the same in both the systems. The gross material elements or the elements which are perceptible to the senses proceed from subtle elements which are imperceptible to the senses. These elements, according to the Sānkhya, are derived from Nature as their last cause, and, according to the Vedanta, from Avidyā or nescience or ignorance.

The work of evolution is as instantaneous and rapid as a flash of lightning. According to the Vedanta, Brahma, overspread with illusion, manifests itself in three orders of intelligence in three states of experience; (1) *Içwara* in the state of *sushupti* or dreamless sleep; (2) *Hiranyagarbha* or *Taijasa* in the state of dreaming sleep *(svapna)*; (3) *Vaishwánara* or *Virát Purusha* in the state of waking *(Jágrat)*.

There are three classes of bodies for these three orders of intelligence; the *Kárana Sharira* (casual body) and the *Anandamaya kosha* (sac of bliss) of *Içwara*; *Sukshma Sharira* or tenuous involucra or subtle bodies of *Jivatmas* (transmigrating spirits). This *Sukshma Sharira* consists of three sacs laid one over the other, *viz.*, the cognitional *i.e.*, the intellect and the organs of senses; the sensorial, the organs of action and common senses; the respiratory or five vital airs. *Sthula Sharira* is the gross body of the transmigrating spirits or the *Annarasamaya-Kosha* or the nutrimentitious wrapper. Clothed with these five successive wrappers or sheaths the impersonal self manifests itself as various sentiencies, as god, man, beast.

## CHAPTER IV.

### THE THREE GUNAS OR THE UNIVERSAL TENDENCIES OF NATURE.

THE three Gunas or the universal tendencies of Nature form a most important factor in the metaphysical system of the Hindus. The great First Cause is the Infinite, Incomprehensible, Self-existing Being from whom all spiritual and material matter is derived and from whom proceeds the universe. Being immaterial, he is above corruption; being invisible he can have no form or quality; but what we behold is his works. The entire universe, consisting of animate and inanimate creations, has emerged out of God, and into Him, it will, in course of time, merge. He is the Absolute Reality and all things present to our consciousness are its phenomena or shows. God is the neumenon, and the universe before us is phenomenal. The Absolute Real God manifests Himself as related for creating the universe, which is called His Mayā. As the beautiful luminary the sun casts its rays of light upon millions of pools of water and reflects himself at the same moment on each of them, so are our souls the manifestations of the Divine Being. The creative power or energy of God is Prakriti or Nature—the material cause of the universe. It is blind and purposeless, without form or parts, is eternal, material, universal, forming for itself yet undeveloped being from which proceeds the visible world. In this creative energy of God, the material cause of the universe, we find, on an analysis, three universal tendencies which are named by the Rishis the three *Gunas.* The action of these universal tendencies is not only visible in the nature of man, but it is equally so in the lower order of animate beings as well as in inanimate creation. We find three universal tendencies or forces acting on the face of creation. There is the chaotic or disorganising tendency which leads everything into confusion; there is the isolating tendency, by which every object tries to secure an individual position of its own and there is the harmonizing tendency by which every object gravitates to a centre in creation and which tries to bring all objects of creation into one universal order. Thus in creation there is one disorganizing tendency, one isolating tendency and one organizing tendency. These three universal tendencies are inherent in creation, both animate and inanimate, and every form of growth is dependent upon the working of these tendencies. They are not the materials or ingredients which form all the objects of nature, but the laws that regulate their creation—the inherent energies or tendencies. The first is called the *Tama-guna* or the disorganizing tendency or the energy that brings on confusion in the work of creation and puts obstacles in the way of order or harmony. The second is called *Raja-guna* or isolating tendency—or the inherent energy by which every object in nature struggles to secure its own independence and to isolate itself from the rest. The third is the *Sattwa-guna* or the tendency that tries to establish universal order—the energy that tries to overcome confusing and isolating tendencies and bring every thing into the centre of a universal order. Because the creative energy of God is invested in these three qualities or universal tendencies, therefore every object in creation partakes of their nature. Thus the harmonizing or organizing tendency is called the *Sattwa-guna*; the isolating tendency is called the *Raja-guna*; and the disorganizing tendency is called the *Tama-guna*. These three universal tendencies, energies or qualities regulate the entire universe.

We will first explain how we can perceive the work of the three gunas in inorganic creation. Before doing so we should try to explain the relation of the three universal tendencies or principles of creation. In Hindu cosmogony the three gunas lie in a state of equilibrium in Prakriti or the material cause of the universe. There is no action possible when these three are in a balanced state. Suppose, a piece of stone is tied with three ropes and drawn with equal force and at the same time by three persons: it does not move and remains stationary where it lies. Therefore when the three energies or qualities lie in a balanced state in Prakriti, it does no work. This is called the pure or balanced state of Nature.*

The well-balanced state of the three gunas is Prakriti. The first product of Prakriti

* Thus is it defined in the Sankhya :

सत्वरजस्तमसां साम्यावस्था प्रकृतिः ।

is *Buddhi* or the grand nucleus of intelligence. It is a free, uncreated and uncreating principle which exists everywhere; is eternal, without beginning or end, invisible, immortal and only known by reflection. It possesses no active quality unless when united with matter. It partakes of the qualities of Nature. Next was produced *Ahankâra*, egoism or self consciousness, the active power of Nature produced by the union of matter and soul. This produces the isolating tendency of Nature and in it predominates *raja-guna*. And then the elements were produced—the first of which was ether (Akāsa). The Hindu philosophers came to the conclusion that there is no vacuum in Nature; and observing that air and other elements were excluded under various circumstances from space, they devised, in order to account for the separation of particles, a subtle element or ether by which all interstices, even the most minute, were pervaded and to which they ascribed the property of carrying sound. By its transformation the *air* or atmosphere, the vehicle of sense, was formed; it is possessed of sonorousness, tangibility and lightness. Having much of the active principle it gives the moving powers and qualities to bodies. From it proceeded fire or rather light. And then were produced water and earth. The joint operation of matter and spirit, the active principle, with the five elements, constituted the principles by which the universe was formed: at first as an undeveloped mass from which proceeded by a regular gradation the sensitive and intellectual faculties of man. Thus we find *tama-guna* in crude, chaotic matter, *raja-guna* in the form which it gradually assumes, and *sattwa-guna* in the order and arrangement which forms the great universal order.

These three *gunas* are, therefore, perceptible both in organic and inorganic creation. In inorganic creation the three universal tendencies are thus seen. Take for instance the solar system. The earth originally existed in the shape of formless, crude matter. In this state the *Tama-guna* predominates. Then it takes a form and becomes earth with certain forces of its own. Herein the *raja-guna* predominates. Then by another force it is regularly drawn towards a centre and performs regular and well-ordered movements, contributing towards a grand and regular system. This tendency is called the *sattwa guna*. Similarly, we find the action of the three *gunas* in the vegetable kingdom. A tree, for instance, originally exists in the form of a crude, shapeless particle. This is the *tâmasik* state of the tree: it then sprouts up and grows up into a tree: herein we find an individualizing tendency: this is called the *râjasik* tendency: a tree gives fruits and serves many other purposes for men and other animals. This act of giving fruits has nothing to do with the individual growth of the tree. In a tree this is the *sáttwik* tendency.

It is the action of these three *gunas* on human nature that we mean carefully to analyse. The Hindu philosophers held that the body was formed of the same elements and qualities as those of the world and crude, inert matter, and was only known in connection with, and governed by, the independent soul. This union produced the active power of Nature, "egoism" or self-consciousness (*Ahankâra*) or personal conviction, or the belief that *I am*, by which external impressions are conveyed to the soul. As in inorganic creation, so in organic creation we find the universal tendencies both in men and the lower order of animals. In animals and beasts their brute nature is their *támasik* state. The *rájasik* tendency works in them when they put forth exertions for procuring food, for destroying others, for their safety and so forth. When, amongst some animals it is seen that they do not show themselves as the brutes ordinarily do, they do not injure others—bnt show signs of gratefulness and reciprocity, it is to be understood that in it predominates the *Sattwa-gnna*. On many occasions we have heard of a human baby brought up by a tiger or a bear, of dogs following their masters faithfully, of horses reciprocating feeling ot love in other animals. This happens when *Sattwa-guna* prevails in excess in that particular animal, because by its predominanee that particular animal does not show itself in the way in which others of its species ordinarily do by their brute nature. A tiger naturally kills a human being. But when it rears up a human baby, it surely does so under the influence of *Sattwa-guna*, because it is an act against the brute nature of the tiger.

It is in human nature particularly that we observe the influence of these three universal tendencies or qualities. In men they regulate the relation of the human soul with the body and the faculties and that of the human soul with the Divine Soul. The *Geeta* says,*—

"*Sattwa*, *raja* and *tama*, these three qualities of Nature, O mighty-armed, bind down the eternal self in the body of beings.

Amongst the three, *sattwa*, from its untainted nature, from its being enlightening, and as it is free from misery, keeps the self

---

* सत्वरजस्तम इति गुणाः प्रकृतिसम्भवाः ।
निबध्नन्ति महाबाहो देहे देहिनमव्ययम् ॥
तत्र सत्वं निर्म्मलत्वात्प्रकाशकमनामयम् ॥
सुखसङ्गेन बध्नाति ज्ञानसङ्गेन चानघ ॥
रजो रागात्मकं विद्धि तृष्णासङ्गसमुद्भवम् ।
तन्निबध्नाति कौन्तेय कर्म्मसङ्गेन देहिनम् ॥
तमस्त्वज्ञानजं विद्धि मोहनं सर्व्वदेहिनाम् ।
प्रमादालस्यनिद्राभिस्तन्निबध्नाति भारत ॥
सत्वं सुखे सञ्जयति रजः कर्म्मणि भारत ।
ज्ञानमावृत्य तु तमः प्रमादे सञ्जयत्युत ॥

Chapt. XIV, Verses 5—9.

bound with the attachment of happiness and knowledge.

*Raja*, having desire for its essence, is born of thirst and attachment; therefore, O son of Kunti, it binds the embodied self with the attachment of work.

*Tama* is born of ignorance and, therefore, it deludes all embodied selves. O Bharata, it binds the self with error, indolence and sleep.

*Sattwa* unites the self with happiness, *raja* with work; but, O Bharata, *tama*, shadowing knowledge, binds self with error."

These *slokas* from the *Geeta* clearly bear out that the three universal tendencies or qualities govern the relation of the soul with the body and point out that they have a great influence over the temperament and nature of men.

If we take a careful survey of human beings, we find three forms of human nature or temperament. The one class avoids bad and strives to perform good actions. A man of this class has patience, is a lover of truth, holiness, faith, knowledge and understanding; has no bad desire, possesses a good memory, is charitable, just, firm and devoid of anger, and is contented and without avarice.

A man of the other class has desire, the love of gain, industry and activity in works. He is miserable, insincere, wants varacity, is unquiet, unforgiving and prevaricating. He has no mercy, is rash, haughty, proud, lascivious, intemperate, passionate, changeable and covetous.

The third form of disposition is inert, proud and wicked. In it there is a want of energy or loss of consciousness and love of retirement, secrecy and distraction of thought. Such a one neither believes in God nor in another state of existence.

Thus, in the first form of disposition we find a harmonizing tendency, in the second an isolating tendency and in the third a chaotic tendency. The first is called the *sâttwik* disposition, the second the *rajasik*, and the third the *tâmasik*. As the *Geeta* says:—The first possesses knowledge and happiness; the second has the attachment of work and the third begets error, indolence and sleep. It is knowledge that brings about the union of the Divine Soul and the human soul, and this harmony is the parent of true happiness. It is *Ahankâra* or the consciousness of self that creates attachment for work which takes away a man from the universal order and makes him seek selfish desires. Error, ignorance and sleepiness land a man ultimately in the region of chaos. These three tendencies of human disposition and temperament lead to the various kinds of human actions in the world.

The greatest spiritual idea of the Hindu metaphysical system is that the human soul always strives to have union with the Divine Soul. This communion of the human soul and the Divine Soul—this great *Yoga* is the highest state of spiritual culture. But to acquire this a man has to struggle very hard. His human disposition is pervaded by three tendencies or qualities, and unless he can bring them into a state of equilibrium he cannot attain to this highest form of spiritual communion.

These three *gunas* do not, however, exist severally in human nature. It is not that one man is *sáttwik* by nature, the other *rájasik* and another *tâmasik*. The existence of one *guna* does not imply the absolute negation of the others. They all exist jointly in every human nature. Every disposition is pervaded by the three qualities, but they do not all co-exist in a prevalent state. In one nature in which the one predominates, the other two exist in a latent form. Thus when the *sattwa-guna* predominates, the other two exist in a suppressed state. When *raja* prevails, *sattwa* and *tama* lie dormant.

Similarly, when *tama* works powerfully, *sattwa* and *raja* work latently. It is thus how the *Geeta* says on this point :—

" *Sattwa* prevails if *raja* and *tama* are suppressed ; *tama* predominates if *sattwa* and *raja* are suppressed, and *raja* predominates if *tama* and *sattwa* are suppressed.*"

Thus there is no human nature to be seen in this world in which only one *guna* exists. Every human nature has the three *gunas* inherent in it ; the two lie dormant when the one predominates. A man, however, can, by culture, repress the two inferior *gunas* and cultivate the *sattwa-guna*, the predominance of which brings on the equilibrium of *gunas* leading to the communion of the human soul with the Divine Soul—the highest purpose of spiritual culture.

---

* रजस्तमश्चाभिभूय सत्त्वं भवति भारत ।
रजःसत्त्वं तमश्चैव तमःसत्त्वं रजस्तथा ॥
Chapt. XIV, Verse 10.

The characteristics of the three *gunas* are described in the fourteenth chapter of the *Geeta*.*

The extract below gives further details of the characteristics of the three forms of disposition slightly touched upon by us before.

"When, in this body, knowledge pervades all, then should one know that *sattwa* has been developed.

"When, O chief of Bharata's race, avarice, activity, attachment to work, want of tranquillity and desire are born in this body, then should one know that *rajas* has been developed.

---

* सर्व्वद्वारेषु देहेऽस्मिन् प्रकाश उपजायते ।
ज्ञानं यदा तदा विद्याद्विवृद्धं सत्वमित्युत ॥
लोभः प्रवृत्तिरारम्भः कर्म्मणामशमः स्पृहा ।
रजस्येतानि जायन्ते विवृद्धे भरतर्षभ ॥
अप्रकाशोऽप्रवृत्तिश्च प्रमादो मोह एव च ।
तमस्येतानि जायन्ते विवृद्धे कुरुनन्दन ॥

Chapter XIV, V. 11—13.

"When, O son of the Kuru ràce, gloom, inactivity, error and delusion are born in this body, then, should one know that *tamas* has been developed."

Though these *slokas* do not give hard and fast definitions of the three *gunas*, they sufficiently signify, however, what they mean. In the *Tâmasik* state of a man, his understanding is thoroughly enshrouded by errors and he loses the reflective faculty. Not only is he steeped in gloomy ignorance, but he is sunk in lethargy and drowsiness. He does not know what to do nor does he try to know it. It is intellectual chaos, pure and simple. He is guided by his senses and passions and falls into a whirpool of error. And though he has the higher intellectual and spiritual faculties of a man in him, they lie in such a suppressed state that he is in no wise superior to an inferior animal.

In the *Râjasik* state *Ahankâra*, egoism or consciousness of self, predominates; the self asserts itself in everything. The man is moved to action—he is led to put forth his energy—but it is the selfish desire that is the incentive. He grows so very selfish that he forgets every other consideration and seeks to secure his own end. He creates a false centre around which he moves. By thus continually seeking self he forgets the higher qualities of a man. He is always filled with anxiety—always restless, always jealous, and does not care for anybody but his own self. He is, in fact, a miserable man. The difference between him and the man in whom *tamas* predominates, is that he is active and the other is lethargic.

In the *Sáttwik* state a man conquers all the lower propensities of nature. He does not seek his self, but tries to establish universal order and harmony. It is not that he sits idle; but he works for a great end. He sacrifices his little self for the spiritual and moral order of the universe. The centre of his actions is not his own self, but the spiritual and moral well-being of the universe. In this state knowledge and true understanding predominate in him and by these he understands the true nature of his soul and its relation with the Divine Soul. When he sees the manifestation of Divinity in every object of the world, he drowns his own self in the Great Self, his own individuality in the establishment of the great spiritual and moral order of the universe. He is happy and contented. This is the highest state in a man's spiritual and moral life. He becomes a *deva*.

As these three *gunas* are inherent in the nature of man, they exercise a mighty and potent influence upon his temperament, moral sense, intellectual faculties, sentiments, tastes and emotions, and, therefore, on his actions. We will describe in the following pages, in the words of the *Geeta*, how a man's nature is affected by the *gunas* and the effects thereof.

The *Geeta* says:—

"The fruit of *sattwa* is good and untainted; the fruit of *rajas* is misery and that of *tamas* is ignorance.

"From *sattwa* proceeds knowledge, from *rajas* avarice, and from *tamas* error, delusion and ignorance.

"Those that live in *sattwa* go on high; those that are addicted to *rajas* live in the middle; and those that are inclined to *tamas*, having the lowest quality, go down."*

There is always a moral struggle going on in man between good and evil. There is one force which draws him higher up and

---

* कर्मणः सुकृतस्याहुः सात्विकं निर्मलं फलम् ।
रजसस्तु फलं दुःखमज्ञानं तमसः फलम् ॥
सत्त्वात् संजायते ज्ञानं रजसो लोभ एव च ।
प्रमादमोहौ तमसो भवतोऽज्ञानमेव च ॥
ऊर्ध्वं गच्छन्ति सत्त्वस्था मध्ये तिष्ठन्ति राजसाः ।
जघन्यगुणवृत्तिस्था अधोगच्छन्ति तामसाः ॥
Chap. XIV, V. 16—18.

tries to secure a union between the human soul and the Divine; and there is the other which tries to spread a veil over his higher faculties and bring him down to the level of a brute. There is a higher and a lower nature in man. The former is devoid of selfish desires and the latter partakes purely of the nature of a brute. The higher nature gradually draws him high on the path of spiritual and moral culture and the lower nature gradually takes him down. There is, however, another tendency which keeps him stationary. He does not rise up in the scale of spiritual culture, nor does he go down gradually: he moves about a false centre of his own, working only for his own self. Thus by the effect of *sattwa-guna* on his nature a man goes high up in spiritual and moral culture, the final end of which is Yoga. Under the influence of *raja-guna* one carries on his individual existence: he tries only to maintain his own ground;

he does not care for others. Under the influence of *tama-guna* he is infatuated: he goes about without any purpose, commits mistakes, and does not like to work. He is merely an animal in the shape of a man.

About the effects of the *gunas* in particular the *Geeta* thus expresses itself:—*

Men as a gents are divided into three classes corresponding to the three *gunas.*

" A *sâttwik* agent is one who is free from attachment and egoism, who is full of constancy and energy and who is unmoved both in success and failure,

---

* मुक्तसङ्गोऽनहंवादी धृत्युत्साहसमन्वितः ।
सिद्ध्यसिद्ध्योर्निर्व्विकारः कर्त्ता सात्त्विक उच्यते ॥
रागी कर्म्मफलप्रेप्सुर्लुब्धो हिंसात्मकोऽशुचिः ।
हर्षशोकान्वितः कर्त्ता राजसः परिकीर्त्तितः ॥
अयुक्तः प्राकृतः स्तब्धः शठो नैष्कृतिकोऽलसः ।
विषादी दीर्घसूत्री च कर्त्ता तामस उच्यते ॥

Chap. XVIII, V. 26—28.

"A *râjasik* agent is he who is full of attachments, who desires for the fruit of actions, who is covetous, cruel and impure, and who is subject to both joy and sorrow.

"A *tâmasik* agent is he who is devoid of application, who is without discernment, obstinate, deceitful, malicious, idle, desponding and procrastinating."

The actions of men are also divided into three classes according to the nature of the three *gunas*.*

"*Sâttwik* action is that which is prescribed in the Shastras, which is performed without attachment, desire or aversion and is

---

* नियतं सङ्गरहितमरागद्वेषतः कृतम् ।
अफलप्रेप्सुना कर्म्म यत्तत्सात्त्विकमुच्यते ॥
यत्तु कामेप्सुना कर्म्म साहङ्कारेण वा पुनः ।
क्रियते बहुलायासं तद्राजसमुदाहृतम् ॥
अनुबन्धं क्षयं हिंसामनपेक्ष्य च पौरुषम् ।
मोहादारभ्यते कर्म्म यत्तत्तामसमुच्यते ॥

Chap. XVIII, V. 23—25.

without the desire for any fruit by the performer.

"*Râjasik* action is that which is attended with great trouble and which is performed by one who desires for the fruit of action and who is filled with egoism.

"*Tâmasik* action is that which is performed from delusion, without regard to consequences, and with one's own loss and injury as well as those of others."

It is impossible in this world for a man to abandon action. The state of inaction is a psychological and physical impossibility. The *Geeta* says that "actions cannot be absolutely abandoned by man. Body, mind, physical organs, vital breaths, and the senses are the five causes of action. When the physical nature of man stops, his mind is working, his vital breaths are working. Knowledge, the object of knowledge, and the knower form the threefold complements of action." Chap. XVII, V. 18.

Impelled by the three *gunas*, man always performs actions. Therefore "knowledge, action and agent have a threefold enumeration according to the difference of qualities." The *Geeta* thus describes the threefold knowledge :*

"*Sâttwik* knowledge is that by which one Eternal Substance, undivided in the divided, is seen in all things.

"*Râjasik* knowledge is that which sees various essences in different things on account of their separateness.

"*Tdmasik* knowledge is that which sees

---

* सर्व्वभूतेषु येनैकं भावमव्ययमीक्षते ।
अविभक्तं विभक्तेषु तज्ज्ञानं विद्धि सात्त्विकम् ॥
पृथक्त्वेन तु यज्ज्ञानं नानाभावान् पृथग्विधान् ।
वेत्ति सर्व्वेषु भूतेषु तज्ज्ञानं विद्धि राजसम् ॥
यत्तु कृत्स्नवदेकस्मिन् कार्य्ये सक्तमहैतुकम् ।
अतत्त्वार्थवदल्पञ्च तत्तामसमुदाहृतम् ॥

Chap. XVIII, V. 20—22.

each single object as if it were the whole, which is without reason and without truth, and which is mean and low."

The three *gunas* exert their influence upon the tastes and sentiments of men also. Their influence is shown in the very food they take, in the various works of life which they do, in the various forms of faith prevalent among them, and even in the religious rites and ceremonies which they perform. In fact, whatever a man does, or thinks of, is the outcome of these three universal tendencies either jointly or severally. We will begin with the food which every man is bound to take. The *Geeta** says on this subject :—

---

* आयुः सत्त्वबलारोग्यसुखप्रीतिविवर्द्धनाः ।
रस्याः स्निग्धाः स्थिरा हृद्या आहाराः सात्त्विकप्रियाः ॥
कट्वम्ललवणात्युष्णतीक्ष्णरूक्षविदाहिनः ।
आहारा राजसस्येष्टा दुःखशोकामयप्रदाः ॥

"The food that increases longevity, energy, strength, health, well-being and joy, and which is juicy, cooling, nutritive and agreeable is liked by men in whom *sattwa* predominates.

"The food which is bitter, sour, salted, over-hot, pungent, dry and burning and which produces pain, grief and disease is desired by a man of *râjasik* temperament.

"The food which is cold, dry, stinky, corrupt, filthy and a refuse, is liked by *Támasik* men."

The experiences of spiritually-minded men in our country have testified to the fact that the nature and quality of food has greatly to do with the spiritual culture of man.

The *Geeta* next expresses itself thus about the religious rites and ceremonies of men.

---

यातयामं गतरसं पूतिपर्य्युषितञ्च यत् ।
उच्छिष्टमपि चामेध्यं भोजनं तामसप्रियम् ॥

Chap. XVII, V. 8—10.

Even when men perform various religious ceremonies laid down in the scriptures and practise hard austerities, which seemingly appear to be all of a pure nature and which generally good and pious people celebrate in this world, they are not freed from the action of the three gunas.* The *Geeta* says:—

11. A *sáttwik* sacrifice is one, which, being prescribed by the Shástras, is performed by a man who desires no fruit from it and who performs it by believing it only to be a duty.

12. But, O chief of the Bhárata race, a *rájasik* sacrifice is that which is performed

---

* अफलाकाङ्क्षिभिर्यज्ञो विधिदिष्टो य इज्यते ।
यष्टव्यमेवेति मनः समाधाय स सात्त्विकः ॥
अभिसन्धाय तु फलं दम्भार्थमपि चैव यत् ।
इज्यते भरतश्रेष्ठ तं यज्ञं विद्धि राजसम् ॥
विधिहीनमसृष्टान्नं मन्त्रहीनमदक्षिणम् ।
श्रद्धाविरहितं यज्ञं तामसं परिचक्षते ॥

Chap XVII, V. 11—13.

in expectation of recieving fruits from it and for an ostentatious show.

13. And a *tâmasik* sacrifice is that which is performed against the ordinances of the Shástras in which food is not distributed, Mantras are not recited, fees are not paid to the assisting priests and which is void of faith.

About penances the *Geeta* says :—*

17. A *sâttwik* penance is that in which the three-fold penance is performed with perfect faith, with devotion and without desire for fruit.

---

* श्रद्धया परया तप्तं तपस्तत्त्रिविधं नरैः ।
अफलाकाङ्क्षिभिर्युक्तैः सात्त्विकं परिचक्षते ॥
सत्कारमानपूजार्थं तपोदम्भेन चैव यत् ।
क्रियते तदिह प्रोक्तं राजसं चलमध्रुवम् ॥
मूढग्राहेणात्मनो यत्पीड़या क्रियते तपः ।
परस्योत्सादनार्थं वा तत्तामसमुदाहृतम् ॥
Chap. XVII, V. 17—19.

18. A *râjasik* penance is that which is performed with hypocrisy for gaining respect, honour and reverence and which is unsuitable and transient.

19. A *tâmasik* penance is that which is performed under a deluded belief and with torture to one's self and for the destruction of another.

The *Geeta* again says touching gifts or donations* :—

20. A *sâttwik* gift is that which is given because it ought to be given; it is given to one who cannot return it in any away; it is

---

* दातव्यमिति यद्दानं दीयतेऽनुपकारिणे ।
देशे काले च पात्रे च तद्दानं सात्त्विकं स्मृतम् ॥
यत्तु प्रत्युपकारार्थं फलमुद्दिश्य वा पुनः ।
दीयते च परिक्लिष्टं तद्दानं राजसं स्मृतम् ॥
अदेशकाले यद्दानमपात्रेभ्यश्च दीयते ।
असत्कृतमवज्ञातं तत्तामसमुदाहृतम् ॥

Chap. XVII, V. 20—22.

so given in a proper place, at a proper time and to a proper person.

21. A *râjasik* gift is that which is given reluctantly, in return of some sort of service or benefit and with an eye to fruit.

22. A *tâmasik* gift is that which is given without respect and with contempt to an unworthy object, in an improper place and at an improper hour.

Thus we see that even in those acts which pass as good and religious these three gunas have their own play.

We will next describe their action upon the intellectual and mental faculties of men. The Hindu metaphysicians understood intellectual faculties by the word *buddhi*. According to the Hindu metaphysical system, the soul, when existing in the body, is encased in a succession of sheaths; the first is the interior sheath and consists of *buddhi* associated with the organs of perception; the second consists of *manas* associated with the organs of action;

and the third of vital airs together with the organs of action. These three sheaths constitute the subtile body of the soul. The fourth and the exterior sheath of the soul is composed of gross elements. The *Geeta* thus determines the position of *buddhi* and *manas* in the constitution of man.*

Says the *Geeta* :—

42. It is said, greater are the senses (over the material body); greater than the senses is the *manas* (mind); and greater than the mind is the understanding. That which is greater than the understanding is the soul.

The intellectual and mental faculties together with the impressions of the senses constitute what is called human consciousness. Human conciousness is again divided into three states according to the influence of

---

* इन्द्रियाणि पराण्याहुरिन्द्रियेभ्यः परं मनः ।
मनसस्तु परा बुद्धिर्यो बुद्धेः परतस्तु सः ॥

Chap. III, V. 42.

the three gunas. In the last state man is carried away by his senses. They reign uppermost in him and the mind *(manas)* or the understanding *(buddhi)* lies dormant. In the second state the mind governs the senses and guides them to one particular object. There *ahankâra*, or consciousness of self, predominates. In this state *manas* strives only to secure its own supremacy and guide the senses accordingly. It does not care for anything else. In the first state understanding, intelligence or *buddhi* prevails over *manas* and makes it work for universal order and harmony.

Thus the intellectual and mental faculties of man become threefold on account of the three gunas.* The *Geeta* thus describes the threefold aspects of understanding :—

---

* प्रवृत्तिञ्च निवृत्तिञ्च कार्य्याकार्य्ये भयाभये ।
बन्धं मोक्षञ्च या वेत्ति बुद्धिः सा पार्थ सात्त्विकी ॥

30. A *sâttwik* understanding or intellect, O Partha, is that which knows action and inaction, what ought to be done and what ought not to be done, which knows fear and fearlessness, bondage and deliverance.

31. A *râjasik* understanding or intellect, O Partha, is that by which one imperfectly discerns right and wrong and what ought to be done and what ought not to be done.

32. A *tâmasik* understanding or intellect, O Partha, is that by which one, covered by ignorance, considers wrong to be right, and sees all things in a reverse state.

Thus we see that the basis of the Hindu Ethical Science is *buddhi* or understanding

---

यथा धर्म्ममधर्म्मञ्च कार्य्यञ्चाकार्य्यमेवच ।
अयथावत्प्रजानाति बुद्धिः सा पार्थ राजसी ॥
अधर्म्मं धर्म्ममिति या मन्यते तमसावृता ।
सर्व्वार्थान् विपरीतांश्च बुद्धिः सा पार्थ तामसी ॥

Chap. XVIII, V. 30—32.

or intellect as affected severally or jointly by the three gunas. What is right and what is wrong is always determined by the understanding as it is influenced by the three gunas. In the practical field of ethics, we do not meet with the action of these three gunas severally.

When *sattwa* guna prevails over one's understanding, he acquires the highest spiritual state. He has very little to do in the world and his actions do not at all cause any friction. He engages himself, day and night, in spiritual culture. Again, when a man's understanding is over-powered by the *tâmasik* tendency, he does no work; he is steeped hopelessly in lethargy and delusion. These two classes of men are rare in the world. Right and wrong deeds, as tested by the ethical code of man, are the combinations of these gunas. In the practical world, in the every day business of man's life, these two gunas, the *sattwa* and *tama*, have nothing or very little to do. The former represents right, and the latter wrong, tendencies. The moral code enjoins men to follow the former and avoid the latter. But in the practical field of work, the second, namely, the *raja* guna plays the most important part. It is the self-centering tendency of man, the attribute of *ahankâra* or egoism. It occupies the middle position, and as such, it sometimes leans towards *sattwa* and becomes *sattwa-râjasik*, and again towards *tama* and becomes *tama-râjasik*. In the field of business and practical work men are generally impelled by these two tendencies. The ethical code of man is determined by these two tendencies, namely *sattwa-râjasik* and *tama-râjasik*. Any action, that is performed with a self-ful desire in which order and energy are manifested, is the outcome of *raja* guna. There may be certain actions which a man may perform with a selfish motive, but they help the establishment of universal order and harmony. For instance, for the sake of name and reputation a man gives all his money for the establishment of a charitable institution. A man performs religious rites with the desire that people may take him for a religious man. In actions like these he is guided by a selfish desire, and, therefore, they are the outcome of *raja* guna. But inasmuch as they do a great good in the world, and contribute a good deal towards mitigating human miseries, we find in them a touch of *sattwa* guna. Acts like these are called *sattwa-râjasik.* How many men in the world perform good deeds unimpelled by selfish desire? How many of us perform charitable and religious works and never think of a good name or reputation? But generally in the world all charitable institutions and works of public utility have name or reputation at the bottom of them. Inasmuch as all these works, although performed with a selfish motive, lead to results beneficial for the world—they are pervaded by both the *sattwa* and *raja* gunas.

Again in many diabolical acts, which disturb the peace of the world and destroy the lives of men and animals, we find order, energy and arrangement. For instance, one nation engages in an unjust war against another purely actuated by the greed of territorial possessions. They, to acquire their end, destroy many human lives and animals, but display sufficient order and energy in their work. Because we find energy, plan and order in this work it is the outcome of *rajá* guna. And because it disorganizes the world, creates misery and commits error it is the effect of *tama* guna. And both the tendencies prevailing in this act, it is to be called *tama-râjasik*. Such acts are always to be met with in this practical world. The former class according to the ethical code, is called right, and the latter, wrong.

Although in the field of practical work and ethics *sattwa-râjasik* acts are regarded as morally right, spiritually they are not so regarded. It is the *sattwa* guna only which predominates in a highly spiritual state. The Hindu philosophers regard it as a state in which true knowledge or jnána reigns. It is a state in which *sattwa* guna totally conquers the other two and reigns supreme. Self or *ahankâra* is the greatest enemy to spiritual culture—and this enemy, one, given to spiritual culture, must absolutely conquer. Such a person does not care at all for his own self—he looks upon all with an equal eye. It is a state illumined with jnána and bhakti—it is a state of tranquility, peace and pure happiness. It is what a true Yogin aspires to. Any act, that has the least tinge of self in it, is regarded by him as spiritually wrong. What is morally right is not always spiritually right. That act is abominable and ought to be avoided if it has the touch of selfishness although it might do immense good to the world.

As the intellectual faculties of a man partake of the nature of the three gunas, so are the mental faculties and emotions pervaded by them. Thus the *Geeta* describes the three sorts of pleasure or enjoyment.*

36—37. Now hear me, O best of the Bharata race, where the three kinds of pleasure or enjoyment are. A *sáttwik* enjoyment

---

* सुखं त्विदानीं त्रिविधं शृणु मे भरतर्षभ ।
अभ्यासाद्रमते यत्र दुःखान्तं च निगच्छति ॥
यत्तदग्रे विषमिव परिणामेऽमृतोपमम् ।
तत्सुखं सात्त्विकं प्रोक्तमात्मबुद्धिप्रसादजम् ॥
विषयेन्द्रियसंयोगाद्यत्तदग्रेऽमृतोपमम् ।
परिणामे विषमिव तत्सुखं राजसं स्मृतम् ॥
यदग्रे चानुबन्धे च सुखं मोहनमात्मनः ।
निद्रालस्यप्रमादोत्थं तत्तामसमुदाहृतम् ॥

Chap. XVIII, V 36—39.

is that in which one finds pleasure from repetition of enjoyment, which brings an end to all pain, which is like poison in the beginning, but ambrosia afterwards, which is born out of serenity and is produced by knowledge.

38. A *ràjasik* enjoyment is that, which arises from a contact of the senses with their objects and which resembles ambrosia in the beginning but poison afterwards.

39. A *tàmasik* enjoyment is that, which deludes the self in the beginning and in its consequences and which arises from sleep, indolence and foolishness.

Thus we see that the emotional aspect of *sattva guna* is true happiness begott en of knowledge. The emotional aspect of *raja guna* is selfish attachment and that of *tama guna* is infatuation and delusion.

The three Gunas are also applicable to the various faculties of mind such as concentration, etc. It is thus the *Geeta* says touching this point* :—

33. A *sâttwik* concentration, O Partha, is that by which through devotion one controls the function of the mind, the vital airs and the senses.

34. A *râjasik* concentration, O Partha, is that by which through attachment one holds to religion, and profit wishing for fruit.

35. A *tâmasik* concentration, O Partha, is that through which an undiscerning person does not abandon sleep, fear, sorrow, despondency and fear.

---

* धृत्यायया धारयते मनः प्राणेन्द्रियक्रियाः ।
योगेनाव्यभिचारिण्या धृतिः सा पार्थ सात्त्विकी ॥
यया तु धर्म्मकामार्थान् धृत्या धारयतेऽर्जुन ।
प्रसङ्गेन फलाकाङ्क्षी धृतिः सा पार्थ राजसी ॥
यया स्वप्नं भयं शोकं विषादं मदमेव च ।
न विमुञ्चति दुर्मेधा धृतिः सा पार्थ तामसी ॥

Chap. XVIII, V. 33—35.

We have thus clearly shown that the three gunas are the three universal tendencies that govern the relations of the noumenon with the phenomena, *i.e.*, that of God with the universe. They work equally upon the organic and inorganic bodies. But these gunas are to be studied relatively. What is the *râjasik* state in a man is the *sattwik* state in the brute, and what is the *tamasik* state in a man is the *râjasik* in the brute.

Hindu philosophy has clearly shown the influence of the three gunas upon the intellectual, mental and physical nature of man. They have their influence alike upon the intellect, mind and body of man. They regulate the relation of man with God and the universe around him. Thus the relation of the three gunas is at the bottom of the Hindu metaphysical system. The highest object of man is to seek union with God, and this union is to be accomplished by acquiring the nature of God, *i.e.*, the well-balanced state of the three gunas. This equilibrium is again brought about by the development of the *sattwa* guna and this development is caused by the suppression of the other two gunas. This is the grand process of spiritual culture—so many means of which have been recorded by the spiritual experiences of the Hindu Rishis.

## CHAPTER V.

### MONISM AND DUALISM.

THIS vast universe which exists before us is in one sense real and in another unreal. It is both real and unreal. It is real and eternal for the work of the universe is going on in a regular order from time immemorial and it will go on ever in the same way. We perceive in this universe merely the change of forms, places and circumstances, but nothing disappears for good.

Though in this sense the universe is considered real, but in another sense it is unreal. It has no independent existence or power of its own. The Divine Knowledge and Will are its all. It appears as real for ever but, in sooth, it is non-real.* It is said in the *Yoga Vâsistha* :—

---

* सति दीपः इवालोकः सत्यर्कः इव वासरः ।
सति पुष्प इवामोदश्चिति सत्यं जगत्तथा ।
प्रतिभासत एवेदं जगच्च परमार्थतः ॥

"As there is light as long as the lamp exists, as there is day as long as the sun shines, as there is scent as long as the flower exists, so the universe appears as real on account of the presence of the real and intelligent Brahman."

That which exists for ever in the same state and condition is indeed real. But such is not the case with this universe. Everything contained in it suffers change at every moment. Therefore the universe is not real. Even the atoms, which are the ingredients for the construction of the various objects of the world, are not eternal and independent, otherwise they would not have submitted to the will of Providence. They all work in one regular and harmonious order arranged by Providence. And thus they are subject to the Divine Will.

Although the universe has no independent existence of its own, still it is not a mere figment of fiction, it is no illusion,—for it is pervaded by order and harmony." Thus it is both real and non-real. It has an existence no doubt, but that is not independent but dependent. It depends on the power and Will of Providence.

As this universe is not identical with Brahman, so our individual soul is not the Divine Self. Nor it is a material object. It emanates from Brahman and it is dependent on the Power and Will of Brahman. The relation between the individual soul and the Divine Soul is thus described in the *Katha Upanishad* :—*

"Two have entered into a cave situate in the most excellent part of the body. Of them one reaps the fruits of Karma (action) and

---

* ऋतं पिबन्तौ सुकृतस्य लोके
गुहां प्रविष्टौ परमे परार्द्धे ।
छायातपौ ब्रह्मविदो वदन्ति
पञ्चाग्नयो ये च त्रिणाचिकेताः ॥

the other distributes them. Persons knowing Brahman describe them as the shadow and ray."

The great Hindu Lawgiver Manu says* :—

"Besides The Great Soul there is another which is called individual soul, which is born with the body and which enjoys happiness and suffers misery."

It is again said in the *Prasna Upanishad* :—†

"He sees, touches, hears, smells, tastes, perceives, understands. He is the doer and the Purusha endued with discriminative knowledge. He exists in the undecaying."

---

* जीवसंज्ञोऽन्तरात्मान्यसहजः सर्व्वदेहिनाम् ।
येन वेदयते सर्व्वं सुखं दुःखञ्च जन्मसु ॥

† एष हि द्रष्टा, स्प्रष्टा, श्रोता, घ्राता, रसयिता ।
मन्ता, बोद्धा, कर्त्ता, विज्ञानात्मा पुरुषः ।
सपरे ऽपरे आत्मनि सम्प्रतिष्ठते ॥

The monistic philosophers of the present age hold that all objects and creatures of the world are Brahman devoid of *avidyâ* ( nescience ). For how can a second object save Brahman appear ? There was nothing before the creation. Only God Himself existed in his full form. He thought of multiplying himself and became manifold. So they consider this universe, the individual soul, and the Brahman as all identical. This view, however, cannot be accepted fully. Every object in the world cannot be Brahman void of *avidyâ*.

That All-Intelligence Being who exists in our hearts as a witness, and by whose Being and Presence in us we live, is Brahman. He is our Life of life ; He is our self. Monism, tinged with this conception of dualism, is true monism. One cannot acquire the true knowledge of the science of Brahman unless he views monism in this light. The Lord Shiva in the *Kulàrnava Tantram* thus speaks on the subject* ;—

"Some uphold the doctrines of *advaita* (monistic) system and some those of the *dvaita* (dualistic) system. True philosophy is neither absolutely monistic nor absolutely dualistic, but is a combination of the both."

The Patriarch Daksha has also supported the same view. In the *Dakshasmriti* we read† :—

"Monism and dualism cannot be described. Absolute monism or dualism is no good : a combination of the both leads to the attainment of the greatest object."

---

* अद्वैतं केचिदिच्छन्ति द्वैतमिच्छन्ति चापरे ।
मम तत्त्वं न जानन्ति द्वैताद्वैतविवर्जितम् ॥

† द्वैतञ्चैव तथाद्वैतं द्वैताद्वैतं तथैव च ।
न द्वैतं नापि चाद्वैतमित्येतत्परमार्थिकम् ॥

The greatest religious teacher Rámánuja has thus spoken against monism* :—

"Hoping that I will be freed from endless miseries, and will enjoy eternal felicity, I hear and think of God."†

And again :—

"If emancipation is acquired by destroying the significance of the word 'I,' I fly away even at the smell of such a topic regarding this world."

Thus we see that Daksha and other Brahmavadins have held that emancipation is not attained unless one can drive away from his mind the ideas of "I and mine," whereas Rámánuja has gone to the other pole and opposes the idea of destroying the

---

* निरस्ताखिलदुःखोऽमनस्तानन्दभाक् स्वराट् ।
भवेयमिति मोक्षार्थी श्रवणादौ प्रवर्त्तते ॥

† अहमर्थविनाशे चेत् मोक्ष इत्यध्यवस्यति ।
अपसर्पेदसौ मोक्षकथाप्रस्तावगमतः ॥

conception of "I and mine." These differences are, however, very superficial and both the schools are, in reality, at one. By destroying the conception of mineness one dedicates himself entirely to the Will of Providence. He sees nothing else in this universe but Brahman. But by preserving the conception of mineness, Rámánuja wants to prove the existence of individual soul which the *adwaitavâdins* or the followers of monism deny.

## CHAPTR VI.

### CAN MAN KNCW GOD.

THIS is one of the most momentous questions which the Rishis have tried to answer in their sacred writings. All the Hindu scriptural works, beginning with the Upanishadas, the gnostic portion of the Vedas, have tried to prove conclusively that by going through a course of systematic mental and spiritual discipline man can know God. The highest object of human existence is to know his Creator, to learn for himself the relation existing between him and God for this is the panacea of all mental and physical evils. The Rishis have always held that man can know God, but spiritual discipline is a condition precedent for such a knowledge. In the *Prasnopanishad* we find the Rishi Pipplada sending away six enquirers after God for another year of disciplinary exercises, saying,—" Go ye and spend another year more by leading the life of celibacy, by practising asceticism and cherishing *Shraddhá* (reverential) faith."*

Thus we see that it is possible for man to know God, but he must go through spiritual discipline before he is qualified for the task. The nature of this discipline is also indicated in the same Upanishad. The enquirer after God must lead the life of celibacy, that is, he must give his whole-minded attention to his great work—having no family attachments in the world to perturb his mind. Secondly, he must practise penances, for that will still all mental disturbances and qualify him both mentally and physically for his work. And thirdly, he must have *Sraddhá*,

---

* तान् ह स ऋषिरुवाच भूय एव तपसा
ब्रह्मचर्येण श्रद्धया संवत्सरं संवत्स्यथ
यथा कामं प्रश्नान् पृच्छथ यदि विज्ञास्यामः
सर्वं ह वो वक्ष्याम इति ।

1st *Prasna.*

reverential faith. It is always seen that no one can accomplish a task, however insignificant it may be, unless he is earnest about it. Earnestness is the key-note of success. A man must have faith in God and it is then only that by dint of spiritual discipline he would know God.

In the last *Prasna* the Rishi says that God resides in our inner self—and if one can know Him he is saved from death, *i.e.*, he acquires immortality.

In the same manner we find in the *Chhandogya Upanishad* that Satyakama Javala is turned away to tend his teacher's cattle. He was put to such a hardship only for being qualified for receiving instructions in the knowledge of Brahman. This was intended as a period of apprenticeship when he would acquire all the qualifications, such as concentration, meditation, reverence, faith, etc., and afterwards with a little help of his master acquire the knowledge of Brahman. Thus we see that the Rishis felt the difficulty of knowing God but never felt that it was impossible to know Him. They only say that spiritual discipline and a competent teacher (Satguru) are required by an enquirer after God. Says the Rishi:—

"Arise, awake, seek competent teacher and try to know God. The wise say that, that way is as difficult to pass as the sharp edge of a razor."

Texts like these and a thousand others from the Hindu Scriptural works conclusively prove that it is possible for man to know God. It is the highest end of man's existence. The only one thing necessary for him for the purpose, is to qualify himself for the same by a sort of spiritual discipline. Impurity and restlessness of heart are considered by them as obstacles to the acquirement of a divine knowledge. The Divine Lay, the "Bhagavad Geeta," has also pointed out these obstacles of spiritual culture. Mind must be purged off all evil desires and be concentrated on the meditation of the Supreme Self. This is the Yoga of the Hindu Rishis.

## CHAPTER VII.

### GOD VISION.

WHEN a man engages himself in the meditation of Self, he perceives the existence of a superior power in all his mental and physical activities. Blood runs in his veins; the stomach disgests the food; all organs perform their respective functions; the mind thinks; the words come out. In all these mental and physical actions the man perceives the existence of a Higher Power or Force which animates him and sets to action all his physical and mental functions. When this perception of a Higher Force both in the inner self and in the external world grows deeeper, it is designated God-vision in a man. By God-vision Hindu Rishis never meant the seeing of God like a physical object, which a man can see with his naked eyes as he does the various external objects around him. It is the vivid realisation of the presence of the

Almighty Power in his own self and in the world out-side. It is a possibility which they have declared in unmistakeable terms in their sacred works. By continued meditation on one's own self and his relation with the Supreme Self, a man can perceive the presence of God everywhere.

When we think seriously about our self, the constitution of a man and his relation with the physical world, we perceive that the senses are not the agents of all the works that we do, for they cannot themselves perform any work and have no power to determine the fruits thereof. It is the soul which is the direct agent. So the soul is only the agent of all works and the enjoyer of their fruits. As soon as this fact is determined by us we can clearly apprehend that our individual soul is an emanation of the Supreme Soul and we are absolutely powerless in all our actions. There is the presence of an Almighty Hand in all our works. It is He who makes us work and it is He whose presence permeates our own self and the entire universe.

But this perception of the Supreme Power is realised by spiritual culture. When we vividly realise that there is a Supreme Power always present in us, we gradually consign ourselves absolutely to His mercy. We realise that we are nothing. We live, move and have our being in the Supreme Power. We cannot do away with the great power which he exercises over all our actions. We are then constrained to depend on Him entirely. We cannot but then feel that God is always with us. We see him in our own self, we perceive his presence in the actions of our senses and we see him in all the external objects. Our individuality is immersed in the Omnipresence of the Almighty and we are convinced that the Divine Will is all-powerful and it is He who exists everywhere. In this stage of spiritual culture when a man perceives his own self and the entire universe as being identical with the Supreme Self that God-vision is acquired by Him. A real Yogin, a real Sannyasin enjoys this eternal bliss of God-vision in this world.

## CHAPTER VIII.

### SEEKING AFTER GOD.

THE most important factor, in the formation of a spiritual life, according to the Hindu Rishis, is the hankering after God. A man must seek God with all the earnestness and yearning which his little soul is capable of, and it is then only that he can eschew worldliness, envy, egoism, conceit and pride, and other enemies of spiritual life. A beautiful anecdote, illustrating this point, occurs in the sixth chapter of the first book of Bhagavatpuranam. Narada says to Vyása :—

"In that dreary solitary forest I sat under a Pipal tree fixing my soul on the meditation of the Great Soul in pursuance of the instructions communicated by my spiritual guide. While meditating devotedly on His lotus feet, I began to shed tears out of excessive anxiety. There and then Hari appeared in my soul. Out of excessive love the hairs of my body stood on their end and my heart sank in a flood of joy. I lost all consciousness, internal and external. As soon as the fit was over I could see no longer that charming form of the Lord destructive of all sorrows. Anxiously and with my heart agitated I began to search about. Again to behold him I concentrated my mind in a solitary forest, but could not see Him. I grew impatient and miserable. Then while I was engaged in his adoration in the man-less woods that Purusha, in sweet and grave accents, said, removing the grief of my soul,—"O Nárada, you will not be able to see me in this life. Those, whose impurities begotten by desire and envy have not been dissipated, cannot see me. But I manifested myself to you once only to increase your hankering after me. When this yearning for obtaining me increases in the heart of a pious man he relinquishes all desires of his heart. By seeking me for a long time you will acquire reverential faith in me; and renouncing this region, contaminated by desire and envy, you will be recognized as one of my votaries."

This picture of a devotee's life, painted by the celebrated author of the Bhagavat unlocks the portal of spiritual culture. It is not an unfrequent occurrence in the lives of saints and religious men that they occasionally are favoured with the vision of God. In their devotional exercises they, on a lucky moment, come, as it were, face to face, with the Great Object of their devotion. The Divine Light flashes profusely on their soul, and they are immersed in the perennial flow of the Divine Love. This state of God-Consciousness, however, does not last long and they again hanker after Him. This state of forgetting one's self in the majestic and all-pervading presence of the Almighty, is the happiest stage of spiritual culture, and so every devotee pants for it. There is no end of misery and affliction if one loses it after having once obtained it. The devotee, in his miserable wretchedness, asks, "Why my Lord appears before me and then leaves me alone." The reply to this query is embodied in the words of the saint Nárada. The occasional flood of Divine consciousness, coming down from its ethereal height upon the human soul, is intended, by the All-Merciful God, to awaken in the mind of the devotee an eager desire, a yearning, nay a hankering, to find Him out. For it is this earnest seeking—this hankering that paves the way to communion with God. When the mind of a man is possessed entirely by such a strong desire—his all other impulses are gradually curbed—his passions are subdued, and ultimately his mind is full of hankering after God. When the desire to see God grows strong in the mind of the devotee it reigns supreme over all other desires. He gives up worldliness—he does not seek riches and other comforts of life—he is not jealous of others—he does not think too much of himself. All his passions and desires become hand-maids of one supreme desire to find out the Creator of the world—to go to the Great Object of his devotion. He is led by this strong desire—and nothing on earth can stand firm before this divine flood. The man-soul, urged on by a strong dominant soul, makes a pilgrimage to the Divine Soul. Influenced by a powerful yearning the human consciousness is immersed in the Divine consciousness.

Such then, according to the Rishis, is the true ideal of a religious man. In human society the expression is a misnomer. A moral man, one who observes the laws of the society, a charitable man, one who helps the needy, a good man, a kind man, generally passes for a religious man. He is held in the highest esteem by his own community, and is regarded as a shining star to whom many resort for help and guidance. But mere abstract morality cannot take a man to the

Divine shore. Charity will not take him to the Lord. He may be a good man to-day—there is no wonder if he will be quite a different man the day next. There is no absolute security that he will gradually advance in his spiritual life. There is no guarantee that he will steer clear of the Scyllas and Charybdis of the world. His boat of life may, on an unfortunate day and in an unlucky moment, strike against the treacherous rock of worldliness. The world is beset with temptations and perils. Numerous enemies of spiritual life are stalking all over the world day and night. The only safeguard against them is the hankering after God. If the devotee seeks Him earnestly—all the passions and impulses of his mind will fade away—and he will be a proof against all the temptations of the world. This hankering after God is the very backbone of spiritual life. Without it no one can carry on spiritual exercises, without it no one can see God in this life, and without it no devotee can ever experience God-Consciousness in his soul.

## CHAPTER IX.

### THE THEORY OF A PERSONAL GOD.

THE word *Brahman,* in Hindu scriptural texts, signifies impersonal, absolute God, and *Is'wara* conveys the idea of a personal God. Now who is *Is'wara?*—"From whom originates birth, sustentation and dissolution of the universe. He is the Eternal, the Pure, the ever-Free, the Omnipotent, the Omniscient, the All-Merciful, Teacher of all teachers." He is elsewhere described as "the embodiment of inexpressible Love."

These are the definitions of a Personal God which we meet with in Hindu scriptural writings. Are there then two Gods? No—The impersonal, absolute, ever-existent, all-knowing and all-blissful God of the philosopher is the same as the God of love. The Impersonal and the Personal are one and the same. That which is *Brahman* is also *Is'wara.* When it is inactive it is called *Brahman* and when active, as creating, preserving and destroying the universe it is called *Is'wara.* Are *Brahman* and his powers different? They are same when one acquires the knowledge of the Absolute.

Sri Ramkrishna thus beautifully expresses himself on this point.

"They are identical after one attains the knowledge of the Absolute. Thus a gem and its brightness are one. To think of the brightness of a gem, one has to think of the gem. Thus, too, milk and its whiteness are one. To think of the one, one has to think of the other. But this consciousness of the identity does not come until the realization of the Absolute. This realization is Samadhi—( mental concentration ) in which the twenty-four Tattwas ( the Sankhya categories ) are left behind; not even the ego remains. What is felt in Samadhi, cannot be expressed. Coming down from Samadhi one can give only a faint glimpse of the state. When after Samadhi breaks I utter 'aum, aum,' then I have already come down a hundred steps lower. *Brahman* is beyond the Vedas and the S'astras, and is beyond all expressions. There is neither 'I' nor 'you.'

"So long as there are 'I' and 'you,' so long as there is consciousness that I am praying or meditating there is also the consciousness that you (God) are hearing my prayers. There is the consciousness that God is a person. There will remain the consciousness 'You are the master, I am the servant,' 'You are the whole and I am the part,' 'You are the mother and I am the son,' and so on. I am one thing, you are another. This is differentiation. It is He who causes this differentiation. Hence comes discrimination as between light and darkness, man and woman and so on. So long as there is this difference, one has to admit the personal God. It is He who keeps the 'I' in us. Discriminate how much you like, the 'I' does not disappear. Thus He manifests Himself as a Person.

"Therefore so long as there is the 'I' there is differentiation. None can say that *Brahman* is without attributes and every one has to admit Saguna *Brahman*."*

The *Brahman* is one without a second. But it is impossible to love and worship such an abstraction. So the devotee worships the relative aspect of *Brahman* which is *Is'wara* —The Supreme Ruler.

*Brahman* is the real substance or the absolute reality and *Is'wara* is its highest manifestation. The human mind, limited as it is, cannot conceive an absolute abstraction. So whenever any conception of *Brahman*, by a human mind, is possible, it is of its aspect as *Is'wara* or the Personal Creator of the universe. Creation is eternal and so also is *Is'wara*. He rules the universe and guides

---

* *Leaves from the Gospel of Sri Ram Krishna.*—(according to M).

the form and life of all sentient, and in-sentient, beings. A Bhakta always worships God as a Personal God. There can be no worship of an impersonal God. It can be offered to Brahman only in his personal aspect. The way to the Absolute is very difficult, and people cannot devote themselves to the Lord in his impersonal aspect.

The worship of a Personal God is, indeed, very sweet to a worshipper. It speedily develops spirituality in a man—it does away with human imperfections—and takes a man nearer to God.

All classes of philosophers and students admit directly or indirectly the doctrine of a personal God. Religious aspirants have been divided by the Hindu Rishis into two classes, *viz.*, the Jnânin—one who busies himself exclusively with the knowledge of God, and the Karmin and Bhakta—one who has faith in a Personal God and dedicates himself entirely to His service. The former is a student of

Religious Philosophy and follows the process of elimination in coming by a definite knowledge of the existence of the Supreme Being. In his attempt to find out the true nature of Divine Being, he declares,—"Not this! Not this!" He eliminates the changeable and the gross, and gets at the eternal ground—the undecaying and everlasting Soul of all beings. He represents the rationalistic school of philosophers. This class of aspirants, too, though the highest object of their spiritual discipline is to know the Absolute, Impersonal Self, cannot but admit the existence of a Personal God to a certain extent as the Creator of the universe. Creation implies will and intelligence, and this necessarily indicates a Personal Creator. It is said in the *Bhagavad Geeta* :*

---

* उत्तमः पुरुषस्त्वन्यः परमात्मेत्युदाहृतः ।
यो लोकत्रयमाविश्य बिभर्त्यव्यय ईश्वरः ॥

Chapt. 15 *Verse* 17.

" But there is another, namely the Supreme Being, called *Paramatman*, who being the everlasting Lord and pervading the three worlds, sustains them."

It is then only a Jnanin acquires the highest spiritual culture when he sees Vásudeva (God) in every thing. It is said in the *Geeta* :*

" The man of knowledge reaches Me at the end of many lives. But such a high-souled man is exceedingly rare who thinks that Vásudeva is all this (every thing and all things of the universe.)"

The Karmin or Bhakta, however, thinks and works in a different line. He begins with his own self. He is a man and as such has all the desires and tendencies of a man. He

---

* बहुनां जन्मनामन्ते ज्ञानवान् मां प्रपद्यते ।
वासुदेवः सर्व्वमिति स महात्मा सुदुर्ल्लभः ॥

Chapt. 17, *Verse* 19,

realizes his own weakness and seeks the care and help of an all-perfect Being. He wants to purify his desires, his thoughts and actions. He wants to elevate his own self and endeavours to develop the divinity in man. He has love in him, but this feeling is not purified unless it is fixed upon a Being who is the impersonation of pure love. He has a desire for action—but no action is purified unless he dedicates the fruits of it to a Supreme Person who is not affected by it. The more he seeks such a Perfect Being—the Perfect Embodiment of all virtues—the more he realizes the presence of a Great Personality in every thing around him. He sees God in Nature, he sees His manifestation in all the beautiful objects of creation around him, he realizes His great presence and power in his inner self, he feels His great love in his every day life. God is in him, in every thing around him and in every thing he possesses or does. The God of a Bhakta is thus a personal God to whom he appeals in his weak moments, whose help he seeks in what he does and to whose great will he unconditionally surrenders himself.

## CHAPTER X.

### YOGA OR COMMUNION WITH GOD.

THE highest attempt of a man's spiritual life, the Hindu Philosophers hold, is to seek union with God. They are not satisfied with merely knowing the nature and attributes of the Supreme Almighty, but have always attempted to be at one with Him through spiritual culture. This unification of the human soul with the Divine Soul, this communion of the man-soul with the God-soul is called by the Hindu Rishis Yoga. This Yoga, this union was regarded by the Rishis as the *summum-bonum* of spiritual culture. To the modern scientists and rationalists it is considered as a bundle of superstitions and prejudices—a thoroughly unscientific heathen practice. It is a stumbling block to modern philosophers. That it is mixed up with erroneous and unscientific practices, we do not gainsay. Hindu religious life is a structure of ages: it has passed through many cycles of revolution, depredations of time and oppressions of conquerors. Like other legacies of the Rishis it is coated with crusts of abuses. He, who, however, wishes to study impartially the various forms of Hindu theology and philosophy, the various modes of their spiritual culture, must not be guided by the many abuses he will superficially meet. He must go deep into the essence of things. If he wishes to do justice to the religious belief of this great and ancient nation, who rose high up in philosophy, literature and science before other nations had passed over embryonic existence, he must look beneath the surface of things and go deep into them.

We will first describe how the Rishis of the various periods saw God or how the Merciful Almighty revealed Himself to humanity and we will next describe how they attempted to reach Him.

Thousands of years before the birth of

Christ there came a race from Central Asia and settled in the fertile plains of the Punjab. When they came they had very little idea of God and religion. When they settled in this land of five rivers they saw the beautiful phenomena of Nature before them. There was the majestic Himalaya, the blue azure sky over their head, the mighty flowing rivers running to the sea, the stars, the moon and the sun moving eternally on high. These beauties of nature first arrested their infant attention and they began to find out for themselves who created and regulated all these phenomena of nature. This is the period of the Rig-Veda. The Vedic Rishi is just ushered into existence. He sees the sun, cannot find out what it is and struck with reverence and awe he sits down and bows unto it. He sees the storm and does not know how does it come; filled with terror he tries to propitiate it. He sees the beautiful moon and sings its beauties. He sees the rain, finds it useful and worships it. Everything he sees fills him with wonder and admiration. Nature appears to him a great mystery which he cannot unravel. Therefore, filled with wonder, admiration and awe he worships, adores, praises and magnifies every extraordinary phenomenon he sees. Thus the Vedic Rishi sees God in Nature; and he offers the warmest thanks of his heart to the various phenomena, the sun, the wind, and the rivers as to his best benefactors. It is not the phenomena themselves that they worship but the Force behind them, the mysterious something which they can not know. They saw behind the veil of Nature a personal God of love and power. Thus the worship of a mysterious, all-powerful and all-merciful force was the first stage in the religious life of the Hindus.

In the second period the Rishis tried to see God in their own inner nature. From the external nature they withdrew themselves to human nature. They began to know for themselves the relation of a man with God, the relation of the human soul with the Divine soul. They began to think of the attributes of God. The Rishis of this period were not like their predecessors busy with observation but with introspection. His spontaneous God-consciousness has developed into reflective God-consciousness. He has done with the outside world, he has done with the materials furnished by the senses and began the work of philosophical reflection regarding the nature and attributes of God. In this period we find a number of elaborate and thoughtful treatises written by the Rishis called the Upanishads. In this period the Rishi attempted to go to the Unseen through the inner depths of his nature. He tried to unite spirit with spirit, his own self with the Great Self. In this period God manifested Himself to humanity through human soul.

In the third period the Rishis began to see manifestations of the Divinity amongst mankind. The personal God of love and power came down amongst themselves to lead them on in the path of morality and spirituality. They saw the All-merciful and Omnipotent God revealed in men. He came down and lived amongst them as one of them. He guided his votaries by his own character and advice. He wanted to show men what an ideal man should be. He wanted to direct them how they would most easily go to Him. This is the revelation of Providence in history—the manifestation of the Divinity in mankind. The people saw Lord's *bibhutis* or manifestations in the great men of the world. They found themselves as insignificant beings before those great men. The Lord, by His own life and conduct, showed the world the easiest way of going to Him. This is the Pouranic period of the Hindu religious faith. The Lord, in the *Geeta*, thus says about His coming down amongst men.

"For protecting the pious and suppressing

iniquity I come down to the world at various Yugas." The All-Merciful Lord descends in a human form on earth to lead away His own men from the path of iniquity.*

It is thus that God revealed Himself to humanity at three different periods—first through the external Nature to the Rishis of the Vedic period, through the inner nature of man to the Rishis of the Upanishad period, and by incarnating Himself amongst mankind as one of them to the Rishis and people of the Pouranic period. When the Lord thus manifested himself at each period, the Rishis tried to go to Him—endeavoured to see Him. Hinduism does not consist merely in a blind faith in dogmas and theories but in struggles and attempts to know God, and to be at one with Him. Thus we find three means, three

---

* परित्राणायसाधुनां विनाशयाच दुष्कृताम् ।
धर्म्मसंस्थापनार्थाय सम्भवामि युगे युगे ॥

roads of communion with the Deity pointed out by the spiritual experiences of the Hindu sages.

In the Vedic period the Rishis wanted to propitiate their Personal God of love and power by performing religious sacrifices and rites. In the earliest stage of a religious life a man tries to go to God through works. They realized the presence of a mysterious force through Nature's works and regarded it as an All-Merciful Father. They thought that the means of going to Him lay through religious rites and ceremonies—*Yajnas* performed to propitiate Him and they offered Him grateful thanks for the many blessings He daily showered on them. Thus the road to the Divinity was through religious works. This is called *Karmakânda* in Vedic parlance or *Karma-Yoga* in popular phraseology. It means that communion with the Supreme Soul may be secured through works. To the Vedic Rishis these works were *Yajnas* or religious sacrifices—to every ordinary man they are his every day duties, sacred and otherwise. The Vedic Rishis declared "There is our All-Merciful, All-Powerful God, our Father, Friend and Benefactor in Nature. There we see Him in His own handi-works. We can go to Him through religious rites. *Yajnas* must be performed to please Him, to offer Him our grateful thanks—for He is so kind, and He protects us in every difficulty." This was a child-like, simple faith, a belief in the Personal God of love and power. They pondered over Nature's works, beautiful and sublime. They looked wonderingly on snow-clad hills, majestic oceans, flowing rivers carrying down rocks and trees, thunder, storm, rain, the sun, the moon and the planets, and behind each of them they saw a great force, a person quickening and regulating them. This Person was a great benefactor, kind to them like their father on earth, nay greater and more kind than he. Physical

Nature to the Rishis was not opaque but transparent. It opened its material wall and showed to the seers a great force, a great person sitting behind all. Simple, child-like, and innocent as they were, their faith had not assumed any theological form. Their religious belief is neither pantheism, nor polytheism ;—it is what it is, call it by any name you like. And so they eagerly tried to go to this kind Father. They could not but do without Him. To forget him, to overlook Him was a psychological impossibility with them. They performed every sort of ceremony to please and thank Him. Thus the great road, with the Vedic Rishis, lay through *Yajnas*, rituals, and ceremonials, organized by their infant intellect, which all now pass by the name of *Karma-Kánda*. They did not know to give any name to their religious belief and ceremonies. This the subsequent philosophers did. And this road to God through religious rites was afterwards extended to all works that a man performs. The subsequent philosophers, the men of faith, who afterwards flourished, on account of their culture and reflective power, arrived at the conclusion that men can go to God through works, his daily works, religious and otherwise, provided that he dedicates the fruits thereof, without any selfish interest whatsoever, to the Almighty,—provided that he sacrifices his self therein like the Vedic Rishis. While performing *Yajnas* the Vedic Rishis had no selfish desire whatever—they did not know what self is—they performed them spontaneously without any consideration whatever for fruit. They moved, lived and had their being in the overwhelming power of Providence. And every thing they did was for their Great Father, Great Friend, and Great Benefactor. Whatever they wanted, they got from Him. He helped them, He guided them, He led them on in their life. What they had to do was to thank Him only.

Thus they had no idea of self in what they did.

Therefore subsequently when this road was pointed out by the Rishis for humanity, they had to declare for safeguarding them,—"Go to God, see Him, approach Him through your works; you will succeed if you try to approach him through what you every day do, provided that you kill your self, forget yourself and do everything for the All-Merciful Father." This is the real *Karma-Yoga* of the Hindus.

God revealed Himself, in the second period, to the Rishis of the Upanishad through the inner man. The religious belief of the Hindus had assumed a definite shape at this period. The child had gradually passed into youth and entered upon the domain of thought. He began to philosophise and reflect. The child-like faith and religion of the Vedic Rishis took the form of theology. The work of observation was over and that of retrospection and reflection set in. The Rishi no longer adores and magnifies the objects of Nature and reverentially sings their praises. Now he contemplates upon the nature and attributes of God in his own inner nature. He is not busy with the external Nature but with the inner nature. And God reveals Himself to him through his own soul. He does not seek any external medium, he does not much care for religious rites and ceremonies and wholly withdraws himself from matter. He has thought out and solved many metaphysical problems of importance for himself. He has discovered the nature of human soul. He has, through reflection and philosophic thinking, arrived at the conclusion that by which the soul sees form, by which it hears sound, by which it apprehends smell, by which it expresses speech, by which it distinguishes what is of good, and what is not of good, taste, the heart, the mind, knowledge about one's self, knowledge of the sixty-four sciences, knowledge of what is practicable, etc., perseverance, desire, submission, are the names of knowledge and attributes of the human soul, "Inferior Brahma," and are not attributes of the "Superior Brahma which has no form whatsoever." The Rishi, with his awakened philosophic understanding, prays :—"From the unreal lead me to the real, from darkness lead me to light, from death lead me to immortality." He seeks the true knowledge of the universe—he tries to know what is real and arrives at a conclusion. The Rishi says :—

"A husband is loved not because you love the husband, but because you love (in him) the Divine Spirit (Atma, the Absolute self). A wife is loved not because we love the wife, but because we love (in her) the Divine Spirit. Children are loved not because we love the children, but because we love the Divine Spirit in them. This spirit it is which we love when we (seem to) love wealth, the Brahmanas, the Kshatriyas, this world, the Devas, all beings, and this universe. The Divine Spirit, O beloved wife, is to be seen, to be heard, to be perceived, and to be meditated upon. If we see, perceive, hear and know him, O Maitreyi, then this whole universe is known to us." Thus the Rishi sees the Divine Spirit everywhere, in his own self, in his own wife and children, in the universe around him. Thus the God reveals Himself through the inner self—the inner nature of man. The Rishi seeks the union of his own self with the Great self, the union of spirit with spirit. He retires from the din and bustle of the world and engages in contemplation. He withdraws his heart from all sensible objects, from all temporal thoughts and cares. He does not care for riches, does not care for creature comforts, does not care for objective surroundings and endeavours to fix his attention immoveably on the Eternal Spirit. This he tries by mental concentration. He controls all his thoughts and desires by contemplating upon the nature and attributes of the Eternal Self. He finds that desire is his great enemy and self is the rock-wall that stands in the way of his going to the exalted throne of the Almighty. Every impure wish, every selfish desire hinders concentration. He therefore attempts, nay struggles life and death, to conquer the arch-enemy. He loses himself in contemplation. While meditating on the attributes of God he forgets his own self—and finds himself entirely in the Supreme Soul. His soul communes with the Great Soul, his all is immersed in the Great All. His soul makes a pilgrimage, through the Scyllas and Charybdis of worldly desires and passions, to the Almighty's omniscient and omnipotent presence. He finds eternal bliss there, and ever and anon he lives there eternally. This is the communion of the human soul with the Divine soul—this is the communion of spirit with spirit; and this communion is arrived at through contemplation, through knowledge of the Real Absolute, through mental concentration, through a control of the senses, and mental and intellectual faculties. When a person comes to know that every thing is unreal except God, who is Real, every thing is related except God who is Absolute; when he comes to know that the soul within him is an emanation of the Great soul, when he sees the Divinity revealed in his own self—he seeks this union of soul with soul. He sinks his own individuality down and contemplates on the Real, Absolute God through the process of mental concentration. The human, is at one with the Divine, Soul—he sees duality in unity and unity in duality. Separation becomes a psychological and moral impossibility for the Rishi. This communion of Spirit with spirit is called the *Jnana-Yoga* of the Hindus and this is the highest form of subjective Yoga. The Yogin has been able to drive away all the impure thoughts and desires; by his true knowledge, he has known his own relation with God. No anxiety, no care disturbs the equanimity of his mind and God abides eternally in his mind and heart. He feels the all-abiding presence in his own self and he is associated permanently with the Eternal.

In the third period Providence reveals Himself through history. People see His miracles in their every day life—they see the All-Merciful and All-Powerful hand of the Deity in what they do. God comes down amongst them and manifests Himself in them. His *bibhutis* are seen in the world. He directly guides His own incarnations or *Avatârs*. They are the light-houses for guiding safely the vessel of life in the ocean of the world. God shows the path of morality and spirituality to mankind by His own life and conduct as a man. When they see extraordinary virtues and spiritual powers in a man, when they find in him what are missing in them they bow unto him and regard him as God incarnate, as an *Avatâr* of the Omnipotent Deity. If mankind see amongst them one of super-human intellect and moral sense, they cannot but admire him; especially when they are laden with the weight of worldliness and sins, they cannot but admire him and venerate him. When such a person loves them, not in the way as they love others, when he helps them without any desire for a return, when he lends them a sympathetic and helping hand in their difficulty and misfortune without any selfish motive whatsoever, they cannot but love him reverentially and have an implicit faith in him. These shining lights enlighten people, who improve spiritually and morally when they are in their company. Thus people cherish a personal love and reverence for this super-human being or *Avatâr*. They are so much drawn and attracted by this grand and extraordinary personality that they cannot live for a moment estranged from him. They follow him implicitly and regard him as God coming down to save them. Gradually people advance so much in love and faith that they cannot think of any thing else but him; they are so unconsciously led by him that they cannot think themselves separate from him. This implicit faith in, and reverence for, the Deity, is called by the Hindus *Bhakti-Yoga* or communion with God through reverential faith.

This is the highest stage in the spiritual life of a man. The Yogin forgets himself entirely in his reverential love for God. His love is so overwhelming that he sees himself perfectly at one with God. Because he loves Him ardently, he carries out every desire of His with love. Because he has faith in Him, he submits himself unconditionally to His decree. He does not consider himself as separate from Him. He sacrifices his own self at the altar of his Sovereign's All-will. He dedicates every thing he possesses on earth to his God—whatever is his, it becomes His. In short, his little personality is merged in the Great Personality. His wife, children, earthly possessions, religious rites, penances, thoughts, meditations are all centred in Him. He works in the world by His mandate. He has no voice of his own. He does whatever the Lord commands him to do. He works in the world, because the Lord wills him to do so —he gains success, because such is the will of God—he meets with failure, because such is the decree of the All-Wise Providence. He sinks himself down in the Almighty. Such is the outcome of reverential love or *Bhakti*. In such a state he can have no impure desire, because he knows that his Lord does not like it. He performs charities disinterestedly or else the Lord will be offended with him. He dares not offer anything with an impure heart for every thing goes to the Lord.

He dares not eat an impure food for he must dedicate it to his Lord before he can take it. Thus a man finds himself at one with God through reverential faith. This is the highest development of spiritual life; and pictures of this Bhakti, we find graphically described in the Puranas to afford light to erring humanity.

We have thus shown the three roads pointed out by the Aryan Rishis for holding communion with God, for making themselves at one with the Supreme Deity. Thus the spiritually-minded Rishis of India established the kingdom of God on earth. Every road leads to the unification of the human soul with the Divine Soul, and in every form, after a certain stage of culture, it becomes morally and psychologically impossible for a man to estrange himself from God. But all these roads are the outcome of the spiritual experiences of great men. How far are they helpful to an ordinary mortal? Is it not possible for a man to be in the world, to live with his wife and children and at the same time to continue living with God ? Is Yoga a possibility for a man who must work, as he is circumstanced, in the world? This is the question that the Lord Krishna has solved for humanity in the *Geeta*. He declares that there is no fear for men ; it is possible for every man, in whatever circumstances he is placed, in whatever position he is born, to practise Yoga, to seek communion with God. His great teaching shines as a beacon light to despairing humanity. It is the most practical road which every man can follow; it is the easiest cut through which every man can go to Him. Sri Krishna does not ask a person to retire from the world and enter into the thicket. He does not ask him to afflict his physical frame for carrying on penances. He does not command him to leave his wife, children and other dear ones on earth. He lays down for him a means by which he may live and work in the world and be with God at the same time. He reconciles the three roads pointed out by the Rishis and lays down one royal road for men of different castes, colours and creeds. This is what is pointed out in the Lord's Lay *Bhagavad-Geeta.* That the Lord's teachings are intended for worldly men, is evident from the time in which they were delivered, the place at which they were sung, the person to whom they were vouchsafed, and the Great Speaker who gave vent to them. It was at the battle-field of Kuru-Kshetra, on the eve of the greatest battle of the world, and to the greatest hero that those teachings were delivered by the Lord Himself. The Lord begins by saying :—*

" No man can live without action for a

---

* नहि कश्चित् क्षणमपि जातु तिष्ठत्यकर्म्मकृत् ।
कार्य्यते ह्यवशः कर्म्मसर्व्वः प्रकृतिजैर्गुणैः ॥

Chap. III, V. 5.

moment. A man unconsciously performs all sorts of actions impelled by the three *gunas* inherent in his nature.''

Krishna urges on Arjuna to perform his duty. It is the unselfish devotion to one's own duty that can secure for a man final emancipation. He explains, to Arjuna, all the important metaphysical questions, the nature and attributes of the soul, the nature and attributes of God, the characteristics of three Yogas, the three universal tendencies, the various duties of various orders, and then enjoins his disciple Arjuna to follow his own duty, and that, not out of any selfish motive, but for its own sake, consigning the fruit thereof, evil or good, to Him ( the Supreme Deity ). After being initiated into the mysteries of spiritual culture and various forms of spiritual discipline, Arjuna puts to the Lord the following question :—

" Of those worshippers who constantly adore you and who meditate on you as the Imperishable and Unmanifest, who are the best Yogins ( or best acquainted with true devotion )" ?*

In His reply to this most important query of Arjuna's, the Lord gives his decisive opinion as to the means of communion with God—the road to final emancipation—the best suited for worldly men. When a number of ways are pointed out to a man, each magnificent and important in its own way, he becomes, indeed, puzzled and cannot think out for himself which to follow. Arjuna pants after deliverance—he seeks emancipation from the fetters of Karma, he attempts to secure communion with God. Krishna points out to him various ways laid down by the ancient sages and explains them fully. But Arjuna is in perplexity and he, therefore, appeals

---

* एवं सततयुक्ता ये भक्तास्त्वां पर्य्युपासते ।
ये चाप्यक्षरमव्यक्तं तेषां के योगवित्तमाः ॥
Chap. XII, V. 1.

entreatingly to his own master for a satisfactory solution. The Lord clearly points out the advantages and disadvantages of the various systems of Yoga for men of the world, and gives his decided opinion as to the one which Arjuna should follow. The Lord thus points out the advantages and disadvantages :—*

---

* मय्यावेश्य मनो ये मां नित्ययुक्ता उपासते ।
श्रद्धया परयोपेतास्ते मे युक्ततमा मताः ॥२॥
ये त्वक्षरमनिर्द्देश्यमव्यक्तं पर्य्युपासते ।
सर्व्वत्रगमचिन्त्यञ्च कूटस्थमचलं ध्रुवम् ॥३॥
संनियम्येन्द्रियग्रामं सर्व्वत्र समबुद्धयः ।
ते प्राप्नुवन्ति मामेव सर्व्वभूतहिते रताः ॥४॥
क्लेशोऽधिकतरस्तेषामव्यक्तासक्तचेतसाम् ।
अव्यक्ता हि गतिर्दुःखं देहवद्भिरवाप्यते ॥५॥
ये तु सर्व्वाणि कर्म्माणि मयि संन्यस्य मत्पराः ।
अनन्येनैव योगेन मां ध्यायन्त उपासते ॥६॥
तेषामहं समुद्धर्त्ता मृत्युसंसारसागरात् ।
भवामि न चिरात् पार्थ मय्यावेशितचेतसाम् ॥७॥

2. "Those that constantly adore me fixing their minds on me and being endued with the highest faith, are considered by me as men having the greatest devotion.

3—4. "Those, however, who worship the Imperishable, the All-pervading, the Inconceivable, the Indifferent, the Immutable, the Eternal, who, restraining the entire groups of senses, are equal-minded in respect of all things, and are engaged in doing good to all creatures, come to Me.

5. "Difficulty to attain me is greater to those who seek for the Unmanifest, for the way to the Unmanifest is hard to be got at by man.

6—7. "I, without delay, become the deliverer, from the ocean of this world, of those who, reposing all actions in *Me* and consider-

---

मय्येव मन आधत्स्व मयि बुद्धिं निवेशय ।
निवसिष्यसि मय्येव अत ऊर्द्ध्वं न संशयः ॥८॥

Chap. XII, Geeta.

ing *Me* the highest object of attainment, worship *Me*, meditating on *Me* with exclusive devotion and fixing their minds on *Me*.

8. "Fix your mind on *Me* alone, place your understanding also on *Me*. You will thus after death live in *Me*: there is not the least doubt in it."

The Lord then points out to Arjuna the various means for unifying himself with Him, and then asks him to make the choice and to adopt the easiest. Says He :—

9. "If, however, O Dhananjaya, you are unable thus to fix your mind on *Me*, then try to obtain *Me* through meditation arising from continued application."*

Herein he lays stress upon practice and continued application. If, however, he does not succeed in it he is not to despair: another mode is pointed out to him.

---

* अथ चित्तं समाधातुं न शक्नोषि मयि स्थिरम्।
अभ्यासयोगेन ततो मामिच्छाप्तुं धनञ्जय ॥८॥

10. "If you are not able even to have continued application, let your action be performed for *Me* considering *Me* as the highest aim. For by performing acts for *My* sake you will attain to perfection.

11. "If even this you are unable to do, then resort to devotion in *Me*. Subduing yourself, abandon the desire for the fruits of action."

The Lord then summarises his opinion and says which system is the best.

12 "Knowledge is superior to (blind) application; meditation is better than knowledge; abandonment of the desire of the fruits of actions is better than knowledge."*

---

* अभ्यासेऽप्यसमर्थोऽसि मत्कर्म्मपरमो भव ।
मदर्थमपि कर्म्माणि कुर्व्वन् सिद्धिमवाप्स्यसि ॥१०॥
अथैतदप्यशक्तोऽसि कर्त्तुं यद्योगमाश्रितः ।
सर्व्वकर्म्मफलत्यागं ततः कुरु यतात्मवान् ॥११॥
श्रेयोहि ज्ञानमभ्यासात् ज्ञानाद्ध्यानं विशिष्यते ।
ध्यानात्कर्म्मफलत्यागस्त्यागाच्छान्तिरनन्तरम् ॥१२॥

Here he brings into comparison the various systems of Yoga. In our country we find many practising hard physical exercises for spiritual benefit. They, by continued application, try to obtain mastery over the senses. This is also a kind of Yoga. It is a blind application and is considered as a very inferior form of Yoga. The Lord places this form at the bottom and knowledge of the attributes and nature of God over it. He then places meditation or the contemplation of the Divine Essence over it. This is what is *Jnána* Yoga. But He gives preference to actions provided they are performed without any consideration for the fruits thereof.

Here we find a happy reconciliation of *Jnâna- Karma-* and *Bhakti-Yoga*. Unless a man has implicit faith in and reverence for God he cannot perform all his actions for God. And when a man's desires are purified, when a man works for the sake of God without being anxious for the fruits thereof, gradually then he attains to true and pure knowledge. From *Bhakti* proceeds *Karma*,—disinterested work, duty for duty's sake; and from *Karma*, when all the desires of a man are purified, when a man kills his great enemies, self and desire, true and real knowledge, then, of itself, arises in him. Thus Krishna's Yoga is a combination, a happy and inseparable blending of both *Bhakti* and *Karma*, which is the parent of true and pure knowledge.

It is thus the *Geeta* describes a man of faith, a true *Bhakta*, a true *Karmin*. Such a man, such a devotee, is dear unto the Lord. He says* :—

13—14. "He is dear unto *Me* who has

---

* अद्वेष्टा सर्व्वभुतानां मैत्रः करुण एव च ।
निर्म्ममो निरहङ्कारः समदुःखसुखः क्षमी ॥ १३ ।
सन्तुष्टः सततं योगी यतात्मा दृढ़निश्चयः ।
मय्यर्पितमनोबुद्धिर्यो मे भक्तः स मे प्रियः ॥ १४ ।
यस्मान्नोद्विजते लोको लोकान्नोद्विजते च सः ।
हर्षामर्षभयोद्वेगैर्मुक्तो यः स च मे प्रियः ॥ १५ ।

no hatred for anything, who is friendly and compassionate, who is free from egoism, who has no vanity, who is unmoved in pleasure and pain, who is forgiving, contented, always devoted, whose self is subdued, purpose is firm and whose mind and understanding are fixed on *Me*.

15. "He is dear unto *Me* who is not troubled by the world and the world is not troubled by him, and who is free from joy, fear and anxiety.

16. "He is dear unto *Me* who is pure, diligent, unconcerned and free from all distress and desireless for the fruits of actions.

---

अनपेक्षः शुचिर्दक्ष उदासीनो गतव्यथः ।
सर्व्वारम्भपरित्यागी यो मद्भक्तः स मे प्रियः ॥१६।
यो न हृष्यति न द्वेष्टि न शोचति न काङ्क्षति ।
शुभाशुभपरित्यागी भक्तिमान् यः स मे प्रिय ॥१७।
समः शत्रौ च मित्रे च तथा मानापमानयोः ।
शीतोष्णसुखदुःखेषु समः सङ्गविवर्जित ॥ १८ ।

Chap. XII.

17. "He is dear unto *Me* who has no joy and no aversion, who neither grieves nor desires, who renounces both good and evil and who is full of faith in *Me*.

18. "He is dear unto *Me* who is alike to a friend and a foe, in honor and dishonor, in cold and heat, in pleasure and pain and who is free from attachments."

Such is the deliverance of the *Geeta* regarding the nature of a true votary *(Bhakta)* of the Lord. He is the true Yogin, who, even in the midst of the multifarious works of life, always sees the hand of Providence. He is the true Yogin and the true disciple of the Lord, who, in misery and happiness, joy and grief, success and failure, honour and dishonour, can with reverential faith declare, "Thy will be done, O Lord, Who art in my mind and soul."* *Geeta's* gospel is a

---

* 'त्वया हृषीकेश हृदिस्थितेन
यथा नियुक्तोऽस्मि तथा करोमि।"

gospel for the world. It takes every man directly and easily to the august presence of the Almighty if he tries it.

## CHAPTER XI.

### MENTAL DISCIPLINE.

THE Yoga-Shástra of the Hindus is of immense value for its practical character. It lays down the principles of self-culture which only can bring about the cessation of the various ills from which human beings suffer. The Rishi Pátanjali, the founder of the Yoga system of philosophy, has clearly and conclusively proved that self-culture is some thing possible. It is not a dream and has its foundation in our nature.

This self-culture consists of four stages *viz.*—(1) the physical; (2) the mental; (3) the moral; (4) the spiritual. Each stage prepares the ground for the better work of the succeeding one. In this article we mean to deal with the second, namely the mental culture or discipline. This is the Yoga of Pátanjali. He defines it as "the *nirodha* of the mental operation."* The word *nirodha* does not mean absolute suspension of all the mental faculties nor does it mean absolute opposition. It means the stoppage of mental faculties leading to the concentration of the mind which is absolutely necessary for attaining any object which a man seeks.

To cultivate any thing, be it a plant, an animal, a mind, is to make it grow. Growth or expansion is the end. He, therefore, who does what he can to unfold all his powers and capacities, especially his nobler ones, so as to become a well-proportioned, vigorous, excellent, and happy being, practises self-culture. As the cultivation of a plant requires three things, *viz.*, (1) the preparation of the soil, (2) the growing of the plant, and (3) the yielding of the fruits, so the mental discipline passes through three stages. These three stages have been named by Pátanjali as (1) *Nirodha*

---

* योगश्चित्तवृत्तिनिरोधः ।

*parinâma*, (2) *Samâdhi-parinâma*, (3) *Ekâgratâ-parinâma.*

There is always in the mind a tendency to excitement and again a tendency to stop it. There is always the action of passions and other appetites which unsettles the mind. Simultaneously with it there is a natural tendency in the mind to stop it. The author of *Yoga Sutras* describes it thus* :—

" There is always in the mind of a man the tendency to excitement and the tendency to oppose it—the one being defeated or suppressed and the other growing powerful. And when the mind sides with the stopping tendency—this tendency is called *nirodha-parinâma.*"

---

* "व्युत्थाननिरोधसंस्कारयोरभिभवप्रादुर्भावौ ।"
निरोधक्षणचित्तान्वयो निरोधपरिणामः ॥

The second stage is thus described by Pátanjali* :—

"When from multiplicity of objects the mind is drawn to a single object, this tendency to concentration is called *samâdhi-parinâma.*"

The third stage is thus described by him :—†

"When tranquillity and activity are reconciled to each other it is called the *ekâgratâ-parinâma* of the mind."

To explain more clearly. *Samâdhi* or application and concentration are at the root of every success, be it in the worldly concerns or in the domain of spiritualism. If a man wishes to attain absolute union with the Brahman he must have application and concentra-

---

* सर्व्वार्थतैकाग्रतयोः क्षयोदयौ चित्तस्य समाधिपरिणामः।

† शान्तोदितौ तुल्यप्रत्ययौ चित्तस्यैकाग्रता परिणामः।

tion of the mind. If he wishes to be a successful man in his business he must go through this discipline. Without application and concentration of the mind no one can be successful in life. So this is the most important factor in the discipline of the mind.

But for going through this discipline, there must be the preparation of the ground. A man may pursue an object of lust with application and concentration under the influence of passion. To avoid such mistakes it is necessary first of all to make the mind clear of passions and excitements. The mind should be tranquilized and shorn of all disquieting influences and distracting tendencies. It should be converted into a *tabula rasa* or a white sheet of paper to receive perfect and permanent impressions from its succeeding stage. This process of tranquilizing the mind, this process of driving away all passions and excitements from the mind, this process of stopping the distracting and disquieting influences and tendencies, and this process of preparing the ground for the better work of the next process, is called *nirodha-parinâma*. This is the first and the most necessary step in the mental culture. There are two conflicting tendencies in the mind, one to excite passions and the other to stop them. When the latter prevails it is the *nirodha-parinâma*. The external objects always make an impression on the mind. There are always two counteracting tendencies in a human mind, the one to create excitement and the other to stop it.

To make this point more clear let us use an example. A person sees a beautiful woman. Her beauty at once makes an impression on his mind. The tendency of excitement creates a desire in his mind to have that woman. But when he feels that it is unfair to touch another's wife, he succeeds in stopping the unfair tendency created in him. This power of stopping the excitement is callèd *nirodha parinâma.* Thus this step is of greatest value for successful mental discipline which is engendered by the second, *viz.*, *samâdhi parinâma.*

After the stoppage of excitement the mind is in a perfectly tranquil state and is shorn of prejudices and passions. The ground is well prepared for the action of *samâdhi.* When by *nirodha* the mind is freed of all the pre-existing impressions, a man may work dispassionately and freely for he is no longer under the influence of passions. In this state only the worthiest objects arrest the attention of a man to the exclusion of all other useless and minor objects. In this state the mind proceeds from the multitude of objects to one single object. Here the mind is concentrated on one single purpose or object. The will-power of the man is entirely engrossed by the object he meditates on. The concentration of the mind to one thing at a time wards off all distractions and brings on success in the long run. Pátanjali has suggested that to prevent mental distractions and to acquire the power of application and concentration, it is better to dwell upon one truth or object. He says* :—

"For the prevention of distraction one truth should be practised."

He has also laid down various means for acquiring concentration of the mind to one single object or purpose, such as the cultivation of moral virtue, the regulation of breath, the devotion to worldly objects, etc. But according to him the highest cultivation of mental concentration or single-minded devotion is got at by the constant recitation of the name of the Deity with the meditation of its meaning.

Thus like the first, this step has also a little struggle in it. In the first, the tendency of stoppage struggles with that of mental dis-

* तं प्रतिषेधार्थमेकतत्त्वाभ्यासः ।

traction for putting a stop to its operation. And ultimately when stoppage is secured *nirodha parinâma* is got at. Similarly, in the second process, there is always a struggle or endeavour to concentrate the mind on one single object or purpose. In the course of the cultivation of mental concentration the will-force of the man is entirely immersed in the object of meditation. The man is gradually identified with the object on which he tries to concentrate his mind. So the closer is the union, between him and the object of concentration, the lesser is the force of endeavour; and the mind is ultimately reduced to a state of inaction. A Yogin can never be satisfied with such a condition of the mind.

And, therefore, the third stage, namely that of *ekágratá parináma*, comes necessarily after the third stage. This is a stage of action when the mind is the master of the situation. In this stage of *ekágratá parináma* the will-power is self-possessed and not lost. In the state of *nirodha parinâma* the mind is tranquilized or rendered vacant so as to make it free from excitement and ready to receive new ideas. In *samâdhi parinâma* all the ideas are brought to a focus and the mind is concentrated on one single object. But both these stages are defective. The first stage is merely that of preparation with nothing new added to it. It simply makes the mind free from excitement and passions. The second is one of great struggle in the very beginning and of inaction in the end. In this stage, the mind is absolutely engrossed in the object of concentration and the will-power is lost. In the third stage or the state of *ekâgratâ parinâma*, the will-power is masterful and the man works without being affected by passions or sentiments. This is the highest stage of mental culture, for it is the stage of absolute harmonization. In this state, a man forgets his self and acts for the realization of the highest end of his duty. He only enjoys the state of true *ekágratá* who remonstrates with an offender without anger and who eats without greediness. Arjuna was directed by Sri Krishna to fight in this state of the mind. Thus the *ekágratá parináma* is the highest phase of mental culture.

Now, what is the result of this three-fold mental discipline? It increases the natural faculties of a man's mind and deepens his power of grasping. He becomes the master of the situation and nothing on earth can disturb his mental equanimity. He enters head and soul into a work which he undertakes and meets with success in the long run. This is the highest requisite for securing greatness in this world. It is by virtue of this three-fold mental discipline that all great men of the world rose into eminence in their time. To those who do not care for this world but attempt only to be at one with the Supreme Brahman, this training is the first foot-step, without which no one will be able to rise to the top of the ladder of moral and spiritual culture.

## CHAPTER XII.

### SPIRITUAL DISCIPLINE.

HINDUISM is not a religion of lifeless dogmas and theories—Hinduism is not a mere blind faith in rituals and ceremonials, as some would suppose it to be—the real Hinduism of the Rishis is a moral and spiritual endeavour to attain perfection in human life: it is a struggle, zealous and earnest, which a man carries on with flesh and various temptations and failings, it is heir, to become a *Devatá* in this world. The *summum bonum*, the highest goal of human life, the Hindu metaphysicians hold, is to be like God in this world. It is not merely a speculation, that they indulge in, it is not a day dream of religious fanatics—but it is a spiritual and moral truth, which they have realized in life. There are two tendencies in a man's mind—one is higher and another lower, one good and another evil. The former is called *Daivik* or angelic, and the latter is called *Asuric* or demonaic, or in other words the former is called godliness and the latter, brutishness. The former exhibits the relation of the soul, which partakes of the nature and essence of God with the mind, and the latter that of the senses with it. It is the mind and its faculties, like memory, reasoning, etc., that have assigned a place more elevated than that of brute animals, to man in the scale of creation. But they possess the senses in common with the inferior creatures. When the mind, by the exercise of higher faculties, goes towards the soul, it is then that the *Devabhâva*, or the higher tendency predominates in him. And when the senses control over the mind brutishness asserts itself. The *Bhagavad-Geeta*, in the sixteenth chapter, has beautifully pourtrayed the characteristics of these two classes of men in the world.

Thus the *Geeta* succintly expresses itself on the point :—

"Fearlessness, purity of heart, perseverance, Yoga, meditation, gifts, self-restraint, sacrifice, study of the Vedas, penances, uprightness, non-doing of injury, truth, freedom from anger, renunciation, tranquillity, freedom from fault-finding, compassion for all, absence of covetousness, gentleness, modesty, absence of restlessness, vigour, forgiveness, firmness, cleanliness, absence of quarrelsomeness, freedom from vanity, O Bharata, all these belong to him who is god-like. Hypocrisy, pride, conceit, wrath, rudeness, ignorance, O Partha, belong to him who is demonaic."*

---

* अभयं सत्त्वसंशुद्धिर्ज्ञानयोगव्यवस्थितिः ।
दानं दमश्च यज्ञश्च स्वाध्यायस्तप आर्जवम् ॥ १
अहिंसा सत्यमक्रोधस्त्यागः शान्तिरपैशुनम् ।
दया भूतेष्वलोलुप्त्वं मार्दवं ह्रीरचापलम् ॥ २
तेजः क्षमा धृतिः शौचमद्रोहो नातिमानिता ।
भवन्ति सम्पदं दैवीमभिजातस्य भारत ॥ ३
दम्भो दर्पोऽभिमानश्च क्रोधः पारुष्यमेव च ।
अज्ञानं चाभिजातस्य पार्थ सम्पदमासुरीम् ॥ ४

The *Geeta* then gives a particular account of the temperament of the demonaic. It is a fact that needs no demonstration, that we see men around us born so different from one another in nature. These diverse temperaments, in the view of the Hindu sages, are the outcome of the three Gunas or universal tendencies. The question is :—"Are then men to continue as they are born in nature? Are they to be so all through their life? Is there no means of their improving their nature? Is it not possible for a man to change his nature?" The answer given to these queries by the Hindu sages forms the key-note of their system of spiritual culture. There is no eternal perdi-

---

दैवी सम्पद्विमोक्षाय निबन्धायासुरी मता ।
मा शुचः सम्पदं दैवीमभिजातोऽसि पाण्डव ॥ ५
द्वौ भूतसर्गौ लोकेऽस्मिन् दैव आसुर एव च ।
दैवो विस्तरशः प्रोक्त आसुरं पार्थ मे शृणु ॥ ६

Chap. XVI.

tion or hell for a sinner. The Hindu Rishis do not say to an erring man or a sinful individual "Avaunt, there is no salvation for thee." The Hindu Rishi does not declare, "you are not to be saved, unless you believe in this particular dogma that I lay down." No, this is not his theology. His theology is not one of eternal hell and fire for a sinner. His theology does not present a grim picture of despair and hopelessness to a led-astray sheep. He vouchsafes consolation and hope to every erring person. With a trumpet voice, audible to all, the Rishi, from the dignified pedestal of spiritualism, declares a system of culture and announces :—" Here is the way for you all, sinners and virtuous men alike. Follow it and there is the religion of eternal bliss for you. You are not consummate and born sinners. You are not sunk deep in the mire of sin and depravity. Frail you are no doubt, but try and follow this system and you will soon find yourself changed into a god.

It is not what I say from mere belief, But this is my personal experience."

There are three sorts of evil or *Tâpas* in this world with which a man is beset—namely *Adhmyâtmik* or spiritual, *adhibhoutik* or physical and *Adhidaivik* or supernatural. The greatest purpose of a man's life is to get rid of this three-fold ill or misery. For escaping the hands of the second and third classes of miseries, God, in His all mercy, has vouchsafed to mankind *Ayurveda* and other sciences. By a judicious exercise of the various means laid down in their medical science they can overcome the physical miseries. But it is with the means of preventing the first that we have to deal with in this discourse. This is the sole object of the Hindu system of spiritual and moral sciences. This, the Rishis hold, is the greatest purpose of human soul. Material science has analysed matter and the universe and, through a careful process, has gone up to atom and force. Beyond that the scientists have not been able to proceed. Spiritual science has, however, discovered that there is a force, a great force, behind all the forces, and that there is an intelligence and order everywhere working in the universe. It is an All-Intelligent Force that works the laws of the world and establishes the order of the universe. This Force of supreme intelligence is the Omniscient and Omnipotent God. He is the fountain of intelligence and order that we find everywhere in this vast universe. Every object, around us, bears the stamp of His great intelligence and the impress of His supreme will. Every sort of spiritual evil,—mental and moral tribulation,—that disturbs us, is owing to our ignorance of the relation existing between a human soul and the Divine Soul, and that between man and his objective surroundings.

The highest aim of spiritual culture is to have a pure knowledge of the relation of the man-soul with the God-Soul, and that of the moral science is the knowledge of a man's position in the great universal order and his relation towards his objective surroundings. Man is a most important factor in the great moral order of this universe; his ethics consists in his so behaving himself that no friction is caused by his own actions. As a man he has to preserve this order and to avoid this friction with his own kith and kin, as well as with various animals and objects around him, which, together with his own self, work towards the great centre of moral order. *Jnâna* or pure knowledge convinces him that every animal, and every man is of the same genus with him; *bhakti* or reverential faith in the Lord teaches him that every creature is of the same kith and kin with him, for they all form that universal brotherhood of which the Great God is the Father. This relation of man with his objective surroundings involves him in many duties which he must discharge to avoid any friction whatsoever. Moral culture consists in discharging his duties satisfactorily, understanding well his position in the scale of creation and his relation towards other creatures.

Now science has taught us that man has got five instruments of sensation. The external objects are enjoyed and perceived through these instruments. The contact of the senses with the objects thereof produces the various actions that we see in this world. These actions may either help the development of harmony and order or cause friction. Ethical science has its sphere in these actions. A man is a moral man so long as his action does not create any disturbance whatsover in his relation with his objective suroundings. The *Geeta* says* :—

"The contact of the senses with their objects creates cold or heat, misery or happiness."

The real meaning is that when this contact

---

* मात्रास्पर्शास्तु कौन्तेय शीतोष्णसुखदुःखदाः ॥
Chap. II.

causes disturbance in the universal order it brings on misery and when it helps the growth of moral order it brings on happiness. The position of soul, intellect, mind, senses and body is thus ascertained by the *Geeta*. The Lord says* :—

42. "It is said that great are the senses over material body; greater than the senses is the mind; greater than the mind is the understanding. That which is greater than the understanding is the *self*.

43. "Thus, O mighty-armed, that which is greater than understanding, restraining self by self, destroy this unconquerable desire."

There are six *ripus* or evil propensities in a man: they are lust, anger, covetousness,

---

* इन्द्रियाणि पराण्याहुरिन्द्रियेभ्यः परं मनः ।
मनसस्तु परा बुद्धिर्यो बुद्धेः परतस्तु सः ॥
एवं बुद्धे परं बुद्धा संस्तभ्यात्मानमात्मना ।
जहि शत्रुं महाबाहो कामरूपं दुरासदम् ॥
Chap. III, V. 42—43.

stupefaction, pride and egoism. The *Bhagavat Puranam* rightly observes that these are so many thorns in the way of *bhakti* or reverential faith. When the mind loses its control over these enemies they lead it astray and plunge it into the depth of immoral deeds. When these propensities display themselves in deeds, the moral order and harmony of the universe is disturbed. Supposing a man, excited by lust and losing all control over his mind, ravishes another's wife. If all men were thus to behave themselves society will then come into dissolution and the established order of things will suffer deterioration. If every man, under the impulse of anger, kills another—anarchy and murder will stalk over the world. If every man, under the influence of covetousness, steals another's property, nothing will be safe in this world. If, however, men can curb their passions, these *ripus*, so that they may not compell him to perform works under their influence, a man's position is quite safe in practical morality. He is a good member of the community to which he belongs and to all practical intents and purposes he is a perfectly moral man.

There are many external agencies that may make a man practically moral. There is the positive law of the land in which he lives, there is the public opinion, and there is the want of opportunity and means. These agencies may keep a man within the legitimate limits of practical morality. But there is another higher side of the question.

The senses might not come in contact with objects for various other circumstances—but there is the impression on the mind. A man might not commit theft, for fear of law, but he has that propensity in him. He may not carry away another man's wife, but there is the propensity in him. Real moral culture consists in the continued and steadfast struggle in dissipating entirely these propensities through a sort of discipline. This expedient of moral culture is thus described in the second chapter of the *Geeta*.*

"His mind is steady who withdraws all his senses from all worldly objects as a tortoise withdraws his limbs.

"The objects of senses draw back from an abstinent person, but not so his passions.

---

* यदा संहरते चायं कुर्म्मोऽङ्गानीव सर्व्वशः ।
इन्द्रियाणीन्द्रियार्थेभ्यस्तस्य प्रज्ञा प्रतिष्ठिता ॥
विषया विनिवर्त्तन्ते निराहारस्य देहिनः ।
रसवर्ज्जं रसोऽप्यस्य परं दृष्ट्वा निवर्त्तते ॥
यततोह्यपि कौन्तेय पुरुषस्य विपश्चितः ।
इन्द्रियाणि प्रमाथीनि हरन्ति प्रसभं मनः ॥
तानि सर्व्वाणि संयम्य युक्त आसीत मत्परः ।
वशे हि यस्येन्द्रियाणि तस्य प्रज्ञा प्रतिष्ठिता ॥
ध्यायतो विषयान् पुंसः सङ्गस्तेषूपजायते ।
सङ्गात् संजायते कामः कामात् क्रोधोऽभिजायते ॥
क्रोधाद्भवति सम्मोहः सम्मोहात् स्मृतिविभ्रमः ।
स्मृतिभ्रंशाद् बुद्धिनाशो बुद्धिनाशात् प्रणश्यति ॥

Chap. II, V. 58—63.

But the passions fly away from him who has seen the Supreme.

"The madly boisterous senses, O son of Kunti, steal by force the mind of even that wise man who is striving for emancipation.

"The man of Yoga solely depends on *Me*, keeping all his senses under control. His mind is steady who has controlled his senses.

"Pondering over worldly matters, breeds attachment for them; from this attachment desire is produced; from desire anger is begot.

"From anger is produced want of discrimination; from want of discrimination, confusion of memory; from confusion of memory, loss of reason, and from loss of reason, final destruction."

Thus a man cannot only avoid various evil deeds in his life through many external agencies; but he can curb them internally, if he always tries to withdraw his mind and fix it upon some other object whenever an evil propensity gets hold of him. By continued attempt and practice the mind gradually acquires a control over the senses. And if the senses are not allowed to come in contact with their objects they are gradually brought under a healthy control. A man is a perfectly moral man, if he is not led astray by the senses and does not perpetrate acts which disturb the harmony of the world. Thus far is the legitimate limit of ethics. But this is not the end of moral culture with the Hindu Rishis. They must drive away the evil propensities altogether; they are not satisfied till they bring the passions and the senses under the absolute control of *manas* or mind. For this purpose they must have a living faith in God—they must believe that God sees their mind. Their thoughts may be opaque to the world at large but they are transparent to the omniscient eyes of the Lord. As in the practical world the positive law will afford no healthy check upon crime, unless there is a strong Power, a strong hand to administer punishment, so in the moral world, no one will try to extirpate the evil tendencies of his nature unless he firmly believes that his God sees every thing. He may escape the eyes of men, but not those of the All-seeing Deity. To have this living faith in God, a man must know his relation with God. He must know that there is Divinity present in his own self. His heart says, his mind says, his understanding discloses that in his own self there is a higher agency than all the intellectual and mental faculties. To know this,—to understand properly the presence of Divinity in man, and learn accurately the relation of the human soul with the Divine soul,—constitutes the legitimate scope of spiritual culture. It begins from where the moral culture ends. The Hindu Rishi has attempted not only to make himself a perfectly moral man but to make himself spiritual also. He says that all the miseries of men will vanish in the air if he can identify his own soul with the Divine Soul—if his own individual self is immersed in the great Self. This union will put a stop to every form of human miseries. This is the real Yoga. The Rishi sees that not only the passions are his formidable enemies, not only lust, covetousness, anger, and stupefaction disturb his spiritual well-being, but there is another more terrible foe, that stands at the gate of the happy region, that locks the door against him, and that guides all other senses. He lives inside the fort and guides all its servants. He, therefore, enters into the citadel and beards the lion in his own den. This formidable enemy is the *self*. The highest object of spiritual culture is to destroy this *self*, to eradicate it altogether. If this enemy is conquered, anon, all his followers are killed, and he lives in the region of eternal bliss of his Heavenly Father. God manifests Himself in His votary's soul who sees no difference, and understands every thing properly. Every sort of disturbing element runs away from him; his ignorance is dissipated and he enjoys a real and everlasting happiness. And with it His spiritual misery terminates for ever.

The Hindu Rishi has also left for posterity his own experience in this matter. This formidable enemy of *self*, he says, every body can conquer through culture and discipline and this culture is called by him spiritual culture. Concentration of mind on the nature and attibutes of God and devout worship, ultimately lead a man to forget his own *self* absolutely. By devout meditation and worship a man will find himself gradually settled in the Divine Self. He will meet with obstacles in the beginning, for he has to combat against the arch-enemy. But continued struggle will ultimately gain for him consummate success. To keep his mind pure, he must always read scriptures, recording the experiences of great sages in spiritual matters. He must always live in the company of pious men, for it will then hold up, before him, a mirror of goodness and spiritual excellence and minimise the opportunities of his cherishing impure thoughts in his mind. He must follow a good preceptor, for he will always warn him against dangers—and he must worship God with reverential feelings and works. He must perform charities and religious works, sacrificing all desires and being unmindful of their fruits, and he must look upon all with an equal eye. This he can do by practice and culture. Desires gradually subside in such a self-controlled man, as the streams lose themselves in the great ocean. This spiritual culture, the sages declare, is available for every man. For this a man needs not enter into thickets, cut off all communication with the world, and engage himself, day and night, in devout meditation. He must absolutely withdraw himself from all worldly objects and carry on the work of self-concentration. By thus continually meditating on God a man ultimately receives the proper light which dispells the cover of Máyá and shows in the self the Divine Self. This road is call'ed *Nivritti-márga* ( renunciation ). It is a very difficult expedient, and is attended with many obstacles which an ordinary man cannot overcome. There is the other way, which every one can embrace and this is called *Pravrittimárga* ( action ). Man must work and satisfy his duties as he is born to do; but he must cast off all selfish desires. He must do every sort of work, thinking that God wills so, and cherishing no attachment for any thing. For this he must worship God—he must have *bhakti* or reverential faith in Him. By continually working in this way he gradually finds himself in such a state of mind that he can never think himself the free agent of any action whatsoever. He finds himself as the servant of God, in whom he lives, moves and has his being.

The question now is, Whether such a state of God-Consciousness is attainable through spiritual culture and by the difficult process of controlling the mind and senses ? The Rishis say 'yes,' and so does the Lord in the *Geeta*. The Rishis have left for us a record of their personal experiences. Our S'astras are such records. They are the history of spiritual experiences acquired by different sages at different periods. The Aryan sages have not left behind a secular history, because they considered this life a transitory state of trial not worth recording—but their spiritual experiences they have written down for the guidance of erring posterity. This is an evidence of right affirmation. It is the history of the great saints that gives us this assurance, and we have no right to disbelieve it. If we can believe that, a particular battle took place, because history records it, though we have not seen it with our own eyes, why should we not believe that a particular Rishi attained to such a highly spiritual state, because our S'astras declare so?

Besides this proof of right affirmation, this evidence of history, we have that of inference too. By going through systematic drill and physical culture a soldier arrives at such a state that he performs many manœuvres automatically. In this connexion a story, which we read some years before in a newspaper, will not be out of place. Once a soldier ran amok. No body could approach him for he would shoot at any body and every body. The matter was reported to the Commanding Officer. He took his army where that man was standing at an elevated position. Without saying him anything he began to drill his own men. And no sooner in the course of exercise he declared "Soldiers, leave off your arms" than the wild man automatically left off his rifle. If such an automatic action may be the result of physical exercise, why the automatic action of mind towards good is an impossibility? The proof of inference speaks emphatically in favour of our assertion. If a man systematically concentrates his mind upon God, if he systematically tries to control his mind and senses, if he energetically withdraws himself from evil thoughts and evil deeds, if he continually endeavours to do his duty for its own sake, he will ultimately arrive at such a mental state that it will be psychologically impossible for him to regard himself separate from God, and it will be morally impossible for him to do anything wrong. This is the system of spiritual culture that our Rishis have organized for our salvation.

## CHAPTER XIII.

### MUKTI OR EMANCIPATION.

IN Hindu scriptures we meet with various accounts of *Mukti* or Emancipation. Among them four sorts are specially mentioned *viz.*, *sâlokya*, *sâmipya*, *sâyujya* and *nirvâna.*

To live with God in one region is what is called *sâlokya.* To live always in the company of God is the literal import of the word *sâmipya.* To live in God is called *sâyujya;* and to be immersed entirely in God is called *nirvâna.*

When a worshipper realizes the grand truth that God lives everywhere and that the earth, the sun, the moon and all the other planets are in Him, he then lives in the same region. Like groups of small islands in the great ocean, he sees all the regions floating in the great Sea of Brahman. In this stage of spiritual culture he no longer belongs to the earth, though physically he lives there. He finds his residence in Brahman for eternity, and he lives there in the enjoyment of highest beatitude and shorn of fear and anxiety. Thus when a worshipper feels in his mind the omnipresence of God as a real truth and when this idea permeates him entirely he attains to *sálokya mukti*, *i.e.*, he lives with God in the same region.

When this stage of spiritual culture becomes deeper day by day, when the worshipper realizes the presence of the Supreme Deity everywhere more vividly, when he sees God with his mental eyes anywhere he casts his looks about, and when he believes, without the least doubt or hesitation, in the omnipresence of God, it is only then that he is said to live in constant companionship with Is'vara. Such a stage of spiritual realization or culture is called *sâmipya mukti*.

And gradually when this culture attains to a higher stage he finds his own self immersed in the Supreme Self. This stage is called *sâyujya mukti.*

He loses, by and by, his individuality entirely and perceives no difference between his own self and the Pure Absolute Being. In fact, his individuality is washed away by the high tide of spiritual culture. His mind, soul and intellect are given entirely to the meditation of Brahman. This is the highest stage of spiritual culture and is called *nirvâna* or Emancipation.

It is thus evident that though various names are assigned in the Scriptures to *mukti*, it is really the one and the same thing. The four stages merely indicate the depth of a worshipper's spiritual culture. The realization of the true nature of Brahman gradually becomes deeper and deeper in a worshipper's mind and he, passing through various stages, finds himself, in the end, totally immersed in the Absolute, Pure, Blissful Intelligence. This stage, when the worshipper loses entirely his own individuality, and finds his self at one with the Supreme Self, is the highest *mukti* or *nirvâna* or Emancipation. In this stage all his worldly fetters are snapped and he becomes *Jivanmukta*, *i.e.*, liberated when alive. Thus it is clear that *mukti* is one and not many, and *sâlokya*, *sâmipya*, etc., are merely the terms to denote the various degrees of spiritual culture of a worshipper or the manifestation of the presence of Brahman in him. The various scriptural works of authority also, in distinct terms, describe *mukti* as one. It is said in the *Vedântasâra** :—

" The immersing of the individual Soul in Brahman when there remains no distinction is called in the Vedas *mukti*. The terms *sdlokya*, etc., merely denote the comparative degrees of spiritual culture. The true *mukti*,

---

* ब्रह्मैव मुक्ति र्न ब्रह्म क्वचित् सातिशयं श्रुतम्।
अत एकविधा मुक्तिर्वेधसो मनुजस्य वा॥

however, from Brahmâ to ordinary mortals, is one and the same."

It is again said in the *Mokṣha-Dharma*, section of the *Mahàbhárata*.*

"The road in the Eastern Sea does not lead to the West. There is one road to *moksha* (Emancipation). Hear from me in detail."

It is again described in the *Srimad Bhágavatam*.†

"The existence of the soul in its own true form after renouncing the false ones is called *mukti*.

The *Yogavàshistha Ràmàyana* describes it thus.‡

"The true existence of Self in knowledge is *mukti*."

---

* पुर्व्वे समुद्रे यः पन्था न स गच्छति पश्चिमम् ।
एकः पन्था हि मोक्षस्य तन्मे विस्तरतः शृणु ॥

† मुक्तिर्हित्वान्यथारूपं स्वरूपेण व्यवस्थितिः ।

‡ स्वरूपावस्थितिर्मुक्तिस्तद्भ्रंशोऽहन्त्ववेदनम् ।

It is thus beautifully described in the *Katha Upanishad**

"When all the fetters of the heart are snapped, a mortal becomes immortal. This is the greatest injunction of the Vedas."

The author of *Yogavâshistha*, again, describes the excitement of the mind as the fetter, and the equanimity of the same as *moksha* or emancipation.† Again he says that there is no such thing as *moksha* in the etherial region or on earth or in the nether region; the extinction of the mind and its desires is the real *moksha*.‡

The sum-total of these and various other S'ástrick texts regarding the nature of *mukti*

---

* यदा सर्व्वं प्रभिद्यन्ते हृदयस्येह ग्रन्थयः ।
अथ मर्त्त्योऽमृतो भवत्येतावदनुशासनम् ॥

† तस्मादुल्लास मात्रन्तुमनसो बन्धतां गतम् ।
मनः प्रशमनो राम मोक्ष इत्यभिधीयते ॥

‡ मोक्षस्य नहि वासोऽस्ति न ग्रामान्तर मेव वा ।
अज्ञान हृदय ग्रन्थि नाशो मोक्ष इतिस्मृतः ॥

is that it is the extinction of mental desires and of the relation between mind and matter. Having controlled his senses and desires when a man attains to the equanimity of the mind, and when firm and fixed as a rock, he succeeds in discerning the Real from the unreal, and knowing it immerses his own self in the Supreme Self, it is then only that he arrives at the highest stage of emancipation. All his worldly fetters are snapped, all his senses are withdrawn from their objects, the restlessness of the mind and useless activity of mental desires are controlled, and the worshipper becomes liberated although living in this world of men. *Nirvân*, is not a particular region or land, it is not a part of the paradise where a man is to go to free himself from this worldly bondage. It is in the mind of man and he is to perform the mighty feat of the conquest of the mind for obtaining it. And when this mind is conquered he cherishes no longer any attachment for earthly objects and he sees no other being but God, feels no other presence, but that of the Omnipresent. He lives, moves and has his being in the Absolute Self. Egoism discarded he feels himself as entirely God's. He becomes the man of God. This feeling, this knowledge, this stage of spiritual culture is *mukti* and nothing else.

## CHAPTER XIV.

### EMANCIPATION IN LIFE.

OF the four-fold objects of life, with the descriptions of which the Hindu Scriptural Texts are replete, emancipation or *moksha* is the foremost. Religion plays the most important part in the life of a Hindu. The Hindu is nothing if he is not religious. Any ceremony social or domestic, which he is to perform, is preceded by religious rites. Every religious institution or practice is intended to help the growth of spiritual life. It is to the spirit that he pays greater attention than what he pays to the matter. The highest object of his life is to practise spiritual culture. And the end of this spiritual culture is *moksha* or emancipation, both in this life and after. Emancipation after death means exemption from metempsychosis or successive births. It is a state full of eternal bliss when the individual soul is immersed in the God-Soul, when self is immersed in the Impersonal Self, when the *Jivâtma* is at one with the *Paramâtma*. The acquirement of this stage after death depends upon a man's spiritual culture and advancement in this life.

It is only a *Jivanmukta* or one liberated in life, who can aspire to this state after he shakes off this mortal coil. Our Scriptural Literature abounds with the lives of *Jivanmukta* sages that stand like light-houses in the dusky paths of sin and immorality. They declare in trumpet voice and unmistakeable terms that it is possible for every body to be liberated in life if he exerts himself for this great object of a man's existence.

In this world we generally create a false centre of our self. This is the work of *Máya*. This *Self* creates a number of idols which always beset us and make us move day and night around this centre. It gives birth to endless miseries and pains. Emancipation in life means an exemption from these ills, spiritual and temporal. It is a hard work no doubt, requiring the whole span of one's own existence, but it is a possibility. And in order that humanity, weak and frail beings as they are, tossing on the waves of worldliness, may not stagger at the view of this hard ordeal, the Hindu Rishis have laid down an expedient by which every man may acquire this stage in his life-time. It is by the annihilation of self only that a man can secure exemption from this pain. If one can destroy his own self he is liberated in life and becomes at one with Brahman. The following instruction of the great sage Dattatreya to Alarka will explain this point more clearly.

"The consciousness of *Self* is the root of pain and the absence of it brings about its cessation. The mighty tree of *avidyá* (ignorance or ne-science) is in the heart: it has originated from the root of ego; it has the consciousness of self for its trunk, house and land for its branches, children, wife, etc., for its twigs; wealth and corn are its large leaves; it does not grow up soon; virtue and sin are its flowers; happiness and misery are the great fruits; the various relations formed out of *avidyâ* are the water that nourishes it; it is surrounded by a number of bees in the shape of desire for actions and it stands in the way of liberation. How can they attain liberation who, exhausted with walking on the road of the world and subjected to happiness begotten by ignorance, seek the shade of this tree? Those only who can cut off this tree of *self* with the axe of *Jnâna* (knowledge) whetted on the stone of the company of the good, can go by this road. Reaching the forest of Brahman, cool, freed from dust and thorns, the wise attain the most excellent liberation.'*

Metaphorical though the passage is, there is hardly to be found an equal of it in the

* Vide *Markandeya Puranam.*

whole range of Sanskrit literature. It puts the whole question in a nutshell. It is by the destruction of self, which is the root of all spiritual ills, that one can attain liberation. The paraphernalia of *avidyâ* or ignorance, which germinates from the consciousness of self, have also been very beautifully pourtrayed. These are the attractions that bind a weak mortal to the world. And when one perceives the nothingness of all these worldly belongings, he rises high above the temptations and enjoys the sweets of a real spiritual life. This consciousness of self, the Rishi says, can be destroyed by *Jnâna* or the true knowledge of the *âtman*, the impersonal Self, and the relation between it and the *Jiva*, the individual self. By continued spiritual culture, by meditating continually upon the being and attributes of the *âtman*, one attains to such a stage of spiritual culture that he finds no distinction between his own soul and the Impersonal Self. He finds himself at one with his God—his will is immersed in the great will of the Almighty, his being disappears in the real existence of the Great Being, his spirit vanishes away into that of the Great Spirit and the consciousness of that self disappears for ever in him. It is then that a man attains to liberation in life. It is then only that he becomes *Jivanmukta.*

## CHAPTER XV.

### THE PATHS OF EMANCIPATION.

THE Hindu sages and saints have pointed out the paths, by following any of which a person may attain to emancipation or freedom from the fetters of worldly existence. They are *jnâna* (knowledge), *bhakti* (reverential faith), *karma* (action). Although all these paths lead to the same goal, they being the various means to an end, there has been always a fight, rather a wordy warfare, amongst the followers of the different roads. The advocate of one path has always cried down another and tried to establish the supremacy of his own method. The original discoverers of these various means might not have had any difference or distinction in their view, but their followers at least have created broad lines of demarcation that have set one cult against another. Before attempting to prove that all these paths or means are the same, there being no substantial difference between the one and the other, we will first explain their nature and characteristics.

The word *Yoga* literally means union. But the special import of the word is the union of the individual soul with the Great (Divine) Soul. The attachment to worldly objects creates a gulf of distance between the human soul and the Impersonal Self. But when they are again united by *sàdhanà* or religious discipline, the true union or *Yoga* is effected.

*Bhakti* requires the absolute surrender of self to the Divine Will, with one's wife, children and all other worldly possessions. The saintly author of the *Bhâgavat Puranam* thus defines it* :—

---

* मद्गुणश्रुतिमात्रेणमयि सर्वगुहाशये ।
मनोगतिरविच्छिन्ना यथा गङ्गाम्भसोऽम्बुधौ ॥

*Bhagavat*, Bk. III., Chap 29, V. 10.

"I reside in the hearts of all. The uninterrupted inclination of mind towards *me* as soon as one hears of my qualities like the continued flow of the Ganges stream towards the ocean is called *bhakti.*"

To know that everything in this world is *Brahman* and to immerse one's self in *Brahman* or the Impersonal Self is what is called *Jnâna.* Any work or religious rite undertaken for pleasing the Lord is called *Karma.*

The author of *Srimad Bhagavata Puranam* thus defines the various terms* :—

"*Dharma* or religion is what creates reverential faith. *Jnâna* is to see one's self as being identical with the Impersonal Self. Non-attachment to the three *gunas* or qualities is called *vairâgya* (the spirit of dis-

---

* धर्म्मो मद्भक्तिकृत्प्रोक्तो ज्ञानञ्चैकात्मदर्शनम् ।
गुणेष्वसङ्गो वैराग्यमैश्वर्य्याणि घनामयः ॥

*Bhagavat*, Bk. XI, Chap. 29 V. 27.

association from the world ). *Animâ* ( the power of making one's own body heavy ), and *laghimâ* ( the power of making one's own self light ) is called *Aisharya* or lordly powers.

When a Yogin begins to practise Yoga he always meditates *Idam Sat*, *Idam asat* or this is Real and this is unreal. That which is unreal should always be shunned and the Real pursued. Every worldly object is unreal, and so he renounces all, saying,—" it is not real," for the meditation of the worldly objects vitiates a man's true nature. The vitiation of a man's temperament by the meditation of worldly objects is thus described in the *Bhagavad Gita** :—

---

* ध्यायतो विषयान् पुंसः सङ्गस्तेषूपजायते ।
सङ्गात् संजायते कामः कामात्क्रोधोऽभिजायते
क्रोधाद्भवति सम्मोहः संमोहात् स्मृतिविभ्रम ।
स्मृतिभ्रंशाद्बुद्धिनाशो बुद्धिनाशात्प्रणश्यति ॥

*Geeta*, Chap. 2, V. 62—63.

The continued meditation of worldly objects creates attachment in a man's mind. With attachment grows the desire (of possessing and enjoying the object). Desire [when impeded] creates anger. Anger creates stupefaction which again engenders loss of memory. Loss of memory creates loss of understanding which ends in death."

Thus the real *yoga* consists in renouncing the unreal and securing the Real. A real Yogin must renounce the world. He should not only avoid the objects of sense but should bid farewell to attachment and desire. Only the mere absence of the objects of sense does not create the spirit of renunciation. Mind must be equally prepared for the same. A man cannot acquire proper renunciation unless he conquers his mind. He must not only abstain from enjoying the objects of the world but must withdraw his mind and thoughts absolutely from the same. The author of the celebrated work *Bhagavad Puranam* thus expresses himself on the subject* :—

"Even in the absence of the objects of sense the withdrawal of the mind from the same is not completed. He who always ponders over worldly objects acquires them even in a dream."

Therefore the best expedient for a Yogin is to renounce the worldy objects, to discard the senses altogether and to immerse his own self in the Great Impersonal Self. Such a state, the identification of the individual soul with the Universal Soul, the fusion of *âtma* into the *Paramâtman*, is one of perpetual and eternal beatitude. This is the *summum bonum* of a Yogin's culture and he attains to his highest end when he realizes such a state.

---

* अर्थेह्यविद्यमानेऽपि संसृति न निवर्त्तते ।
ध्यायतो विषयानस्य स्वप्ने भर्थागमो यथा ॥

Book 11.—Chap. 27, V. 13.

But this is not the case with *bhakti*. It does not lay any stress on the renunciation of worldy relations and objects. On the other hand, it rejects such a view absolutely. The advocate of the *bhakti mârga* consigns his own person, mind and soul to God. He makes an offering of his own self at the feet of the Lord. He dedicates his own self, his wife and children and all his worldly possessions to his Lord and reserves nothing for himself. He considers not only his own self as belonging to God but views all the objects of the world in the same light. He knows God as the Lord and Ordainer of all and there is nothing in this world which is not His. The Lord resides in all men and all objects of the world. God's creatures and God's objects cannot injure a *bhakta*. Such is his firm conviction and he is not prepared to renounce the worldly objects. He feels that he has no right to renounce God's men and objects. He can accept them, he can love them, and he may be proud of them knowing them to be his Lord's.

Thus *yoga* advocates renunciation whereas *bhakti* preaches quite the opposite doctrine. *Yoga* is related with the transcendental (*nirguna*) aspect of *Paramâtman* whereas *bhakti* describes the immanent (*saguna*) aspect. The former speaks of the Impersonal God and the latter of the Personal God. The difference between *yoga* and *bhakti* is quite of a piece with that between *Brahman* (impersonal God) and *Bhagavân* (Personal God).

Similarly there is a considerable difference between *jnâna* and *bhakti*. According to the followers of *jnânamârga* (the road to knowledge) *bhakti* is blinded with love whereas the advocates of *bhakti* attribute egoism and pride to the former. The superiority of *jnâna* has been described in the various Scriptural works in various terms. It is said :—

"By assiduous exertion one should withdraw his mind from ignorance and engage it by force in following the Scriptures and sages."*

Elsewhere the great Hindu Lawgiver Manu thus expresses himself regarding the importance of *jnâna*† :—

"With water the body is cleansed, with truth the heart is purified; with the knowledge of *Brahman* and ascetic penances the soul is purified, and with knowledge (*jnâna*) the intellect is purified."

In the *Bhagavad Geeta* the value of *jnâna* is thus described.‡

---

* अविवेकादुपाहृत्य चेत स्वैर्यत्ननिश्चयैः ।
बलात्कारेणसंयोज्यशास्त्रसत्पुरुषक्रमैः ॥

*Yogavasistha* 23—8.

† अद्भिर्गात्राणि शुध्यन्ति मनःसत्येन शुध्यति ।
विद्या तपोभ्यां भूतात्मा बुद्धिर्ज्ञानेन शुध्यति ॥

‡ न हि ज्ञानेन सदृशं पवित्रमिह विद्यते ।
तत्स्वयं योगसंसिद्धःकालेनात्मनि विन्दति ॥

"There is nothing in this world which so much purifies (man) as knowledge. The man, perfected by Yoga, learns it within himself in time.

The man of faith, the man of assiduousness, the man of self-restraint, obtains knowledge. He gains the highest tranquillity (*mukti*) without delay."*

Thus the superiority of *jnâna* has been described in various Scriptural works. The followers of *jnânamârga* always say that without *jnâna* (knowledge) a *bhakta* cannot understand the true nature of *Brahman*. Similarly the advocates of *bhakti* persistently urge that only knowledge without reverential faith is absolutely of no use. The author of

---

श्रद्धावान लभते ज्ञानं तत्परः संयतेन्द्रियः ।
ज्ञानं लब्ध्वा परां शान्तिमचिरेणाधिगच्छति ॥

*Geeta*, Chap. IV, V. 38—39.

the *Bhagavad Puranam* has tried to prove this point particularly. He says* :—

"Those who take pains only to acquire knowledge to the exclusion of reverential faith in Thee, O Lord, which is productive of all good, only take the trouble like beating husk which contains no rice."

The same author elsewhere says :†

"Neither knowledge, nor the spirit of dis-association from this world is conducive of well-being to a person who cherishes reverential faith in me."

The weak point of *jnána* is that it always doubts and questions, and that doubt is never

---

* श्रेयः स्रुतिं भक्तिमुदस्य ते विभो
क्लिश्यन्ति ये केवल बोधलब्धये ।
तेषामसौ क्लेशल एव शिष्यते
नान्यद्यथा स्थूलतुषावघातिनाम् ॥

† तस्मान्मद्भक्तियुक्तस्य योगिनो वै मदात्मनः ।
न ज्ञानं न च वैराग्यं प्रायः श्रेयो भवेदिह ॥

removed. Besides it is permeated by egoism and pride. The *jnânin* always takes the pride of thinking. "I have discovered such a truth. I understand everything." Such a spirit of self-assertion is not productive of any good to a *bhakta*, according to whom the proper manifestation of Divinity does not take place in a man when such a spirit of self-assertion and egoism reigns in him. The achievements of *bhakti* are thus described in the eleventh Book of the *Bhagavad.**

"A votary of mine by (faith) *bhakti yoga* reaps the fruits which are acquired by religious rites, penance, knowledge, disassociation from the world, yoga, charity and various other ceremonies. If he wishes, though he does not want it, he may acquire heaven,

---

* यत्कर्म्मभिः यत्तपसा ज्ञानवैराग्यतश्च यत् ।
योगेन दानधर्म्मेण श्रेयोभिरितरैरपि ॥
सर्व्वं मद्भक्तियोगेन मद्भक्तो लभतेऽञ्जसा ।
स्वर्गापवर्गं मद्धाम कथञ्चिदपि वाञ्छति ॥

emancipation and residence in my own region."

Next the contention between *jnâna* (knowledge) and *karma*, (action) is that the former considers this visible world as unreal, while the latter deals with the earthly objects, and makes use of this transitory body for its well-being. The followers of *jnâna* always discard *karma* on the following grounds supported by the Scriptural texts. The author of the *Bhagavad* says* :—

" Withdrawing themselves generally from the ordinances and prohibitions laid down in the Vedas, the Munis (Sages) immerse themselves in the *nirguna* (transcendental) *Brahman* and take pleasure in describing the accomplishments of Hari."

The *Geeta* thus points out the shortcomings of Vedic rituals. Of course we need

---

* प्रायेण मुनयो: राजन् निवृत्ता विधिषेधत: ।
नैर्गुण्यस्था रमन्तेस्म गुणानुकथने हरे: ॥

hardly mention, that the readers should understand by the word *karma* the performance of the Vedic rituals.*

"The Vedas, O Arjuna, relate to the three qualities. Be free from them—by being unaffected by the pairs of opposites (heat and cold; pain and pleasure), by persevering course, by being free from anxiety for new acquisitions, or from anxiety for the protection of old ones; and by being self-possessed."

The advocates of *jnânamârga* always say that *karma* should be discarded for its evils, whereas *Karma-Yogins* hold quite the opposite view. They say that as long as a man holds this body he cannot abandon action altogether. True renunciation, according to them, does not consist in giving up all works, sacred and secular, but in expecting no fruits thereof and working on simply for

---

* त्रैगुण्यविषया वेदा निस्त्रैगुण्यो भवार्जुन ।
निर्द्वन्द्वो नित्यसत्त्वस्थो निर्योगक्षेम आत्मवान् ॥

the sake of duty. The *Geeta* thus expresses itself on this subject* :—

"Actions cannot be absolutely abandoned by man; therefore, he, who abandons the fruits of actions, is a true *Tyâgee.*"

Elsewhere in the Divine *Lay* Lord Krishna says† :—

"Therefore always perform action, for action is better than inaction and your body cannot be supported without performing action."

We have, in the preceding pages, pointed out the different views held by the votaries of the various paths. We will now describe how they can be reconciled and show that in reality there is no difference whatsoever. The true

---

* नहि देहभृताशक्यं त्यक्तुं कर्म्माण्यशेषतः ।
यस्तु कर्म्मफलत्यागी स त्यागीत्यभिधीयते ॥

† नियतं कुरु कर्म्मत्वं कर्म्मज्यायोह्यकर्म्मणः ।
शरीरयात्रापि च तेन प्रसिद्ध्येदकर्म्मणः ॥

nature of Yoga has thus been described in the *Bhagavad.**

"First of all intellect should be purified. Then controlling the mind with that purified intellect it should be concentrated in the soul, the emanation of the divinity residing in the body. Then this soul should be concentrated in *kevalatma* which has no thought for the body. Then concentrating this self in the *Paramâtman* (Impersonal Self) one should acquire beatitude and then refrain from actions."

It is thus evident that unless the intellect is purified, the mind cannot be controlled. And without the control of the mind one cannot fix it on the determination of the true nature of the soul. And as long as a man cherishes

---

* मनः स्वबुद्ध्यामलया नियम्य
क्षेत्रज्ञ एतां निलयेत्तमात्मनि ।
आत्मानमात्मन्यवरुध्य धीरो
लब्धोपशान्तिं विरमेतकृत्ययत् ॥

the thought "I exist, this is my body, this is my wife, etc.," he cannot immerse his own self in the Pure Absolute Intelligence. Therefore by spiritual discipline one should conquer these conditions and then drown his own self in the Impersonal Self. It is when a person has attained this stage that he becomes a true Yogin. The means for practising Yoga have thus been described in the Sixth Chapter of the *Bhagavad Geeta.**

11—12. "Fixing his seat firmly on a clean spot, neither too high nor too low, and spreading over it a piece of cloth, deer-skin and Kusha grass,—there seated on that seat,

---

* शुची देशे प्रतिष्ठाप्य स्थिरमासनमात्मनः ।
नात्युच्छ्रितं नातिनीचं चैलाजिनकुशोत्तरम् ॥
तत्रैकाग्रं मनः कृत्वा यतचित्तेन्द्रियक्रियः ।
उपविश्यासने युञ्ज्याद्योगमात्मविशुद्धये ॥
समं कायशिरोग्रीवं धारयन्नचलं स्थिरः ।
संप्रेक्ष्य नासिकाग्रं स्वं दिशश्चानवलोकयन् ॥

*Geeta*, Chap VI, V 11—13.

with his mind fixed on one point, and restraining his mind and senses, one should practise contemplation for the purification of his self.

13. "Holding his body, head and neck even, unmoved and steady, and fixing his sight on the tip of his own nose, and without looking about in all directions."

The attainments of a Yogin are thus described elsewhere in the same chapter.*

27. "Thus constantly devoting his self to abstraction, a Yogin, being freed from sin, easily achieves the supreme happiness—namely the contact with *Brahman*.

28. "To such a Yogin whose mind is in peace, whose passions have been suppressed, who has become one with *Brahman*, and who

---

* प्रशान्तमनसं ह्येनं योगिनं सुखमुत्तमम् ।
उपैति शान्तरजसं ब्रह्मभूतमकल्मषम् ॥
युञ्जन्नेवं सदात्मानं योगी विगतकल्मषः ।
सुखेन ब्रह्मसंस्पर्शमत्यन्तं सुखमश्नुते ॥

*Geeta*, Chap. VI, V 27–28.

is free from sin, highest felicity, indeed, comes by itself."

This is the true Yoga, which, removing all impediments, brings about the fusion of the individual soul into the Supreme Soul—the union of the *âtman* with the *Paramâtman*.

The true character of *bhakti*, however, is to dedicate one's mind, soul, body, senses, organs, family, children and all the belongings of the world, to God. It is thus described in the *Bhagavad Puranam** :—

" Transcending *mâyâ* ( illusion ), identical with the three *gunas* or qualities, *bhakti* draws a man towards me."

Therefore *bhakti* is designated the supreme expedient. Thus the functions of both *yoga* and *bhakti* are the same. The former, removing all obstacles, unites the

* स एव भक्तियोगाख्य आत्यन्तिक: उदाहृत: ।
येनातिव्रज्य त्रिगुणां मद्भावायोपपद्यते ॥

individual soul with the Supreme Soul. And so does the latter, knowing God as the be-all and end-all of existence, and dedicating unto Him every thing a man possesses.

When a worshipper realizes the presence of *Brahman* in his heart, it is then that he is said to have acquired *bhakti* or reverential faith. *Bhakti* sees the entire universe as God's own, while *yoga* realizes the presence of the Supreme Soul everywhere. Thus, in reality, there is no difference between *yoga* and *bhakti*.

Similarly *jnâna* and *bhakti* are the same. *Jnâna* finds out the Real from the unreal. It discovers the religious truths which *bhakti* carries out into practice. A man devoted to God simultaneously acquires with reverential faith, the realization of the being of Is'wara and the spirit of disassociation from the world. It is thus said in the *Bhagavad Puranam*.

"As a man while taking his food simultaneously acquires, with each morsel, nourishment, pleasure and the satisfaction of thirst, so a person who dedicates himself unto God, simultaneously acquires *bhakti* ( reverential faith ), the perception of the presence of God and *vairâgya* ( the spirit of disassociation )."*

Thus there is no real difference between true knowledge and reverential faith.

Let us now examine the relative merit of *jnâna* and *karma*. The latter carries into action the thoughts which the former begets in one's mind. The very existence of the organs of sense, of the objects of their enjoyment and of the elements, urges on the necessity of action. If men had no necessity of action then they would not have been born with the organs of sense and various external objects. The followers of *jnâna mârga* hold that

---

* भक्तिः परेशानुभवो विरक्तिरन्यत्र चैषत्रिक एककालः ।
प्रपद्यमानस्य यथाश्नतः स्युस्तुष्टिः पुष्टिः क्षुदपायोऽनुघासम् ॥

action and inaction are diametrically opposite to each other, but, in reality, they are the same. The celebrated work *Bhagavad Geeta* shows no difference between the two. The real Yogin is the person who engages in action without desiring for the fruits of the same. The Lord Krishna reconciles the four paths in the *Geeta,** the purport of which is :—

He is a real Yogin who has acquired true knowledge, for *yoga* is not possible without *jnâna.* It is the latter only which finds out the Real from the unreal. And the true *Jnânin* must be a real *Bhakta,* for the more he tries to know of *Brahman* the greater is the manifestation of God's glory and greatness in his heart. It is said in the *Bhagavad* :—

"Dedicating his mind and understanding to me and fixing himself in my religion, one

---

* तेषां ज्ञानी नित्ययुक्त एकभक्तिर्विशिष्यते ।
प्रियो हि ज्ञानी योऽत्यर्थमहं स च मम प्रिय ॥

should perform all actions not for himself, but for my sake."*

It is also said in the *Mahânirvana Tantram*—†

"Being devoted to *Brahman* and knowing true knowledge, a householder must dedicate all his actions to *Brahman*."

Thus we see all the Scriptures have reconciled the four roads. It is for our ignorance that we find the difference.

---

* कुर्य्यात् सर्व्वाणि कर्म्माणि मदर्थं शनकै स्मरण ।
मय्यर्पितमनश्चित्तो मद्धर्मात्ममनोजत ॥

† ब्रह्मनिष्ठो गृहस्थः स्यात्तत्त्वज्ञानपरायणः ।
यद्यत्कर्म्मप्रकुर्वीत तद्ब्रह्मणि समर्पयेत् ॥

## CHAPTER XVI.

### THE IDEAL OF TRUE HAPPINESS.

HAPPINESS is the *sine qua non* of human existence. Be he rich or be he poor, every one, in this mysteriously-ordered universe, is toiling and moiling in pursuit of happiness. The ideal, however, varies with the nature, temperament and desire of the person who seeks it. A poor man, who suffers all the day long from the stings of dire poverty, who struggles hard in this world of stern realities, for a miserable subsistence, who, with all his best endeavours, cannot secure a few morsels of food for his own self and those near and dear to him, thinks that true happiness consists in earning money and making himself thus above the reach of penury. A rich man,—a man born with a silver spoon in his mouth, unused to the hardships of misery and struggles for existence, surfeited with the delicacies around him, and bored with anxieties for the protection of his earthly possessions,—thinks that true happiness consists in being free from these troubles and anxieties. A learned man thinks that happiness lies in mastering all the sciences of the world. Thus we see that the ideal of true happiness is shaped by every individual man according to his own nature and idiosyncracies. But is the ideal, formed by each person for his own pursuit, the universal ideal which one and all can follow? This is a question, the most momentous problem for a human being to solve, that has been sought to be answered by the philosophers and theologians of various schools and climes according to their own light and experience. Varied and divergent as have been the views held by different schools of thought of different countries, there is to be seen one underlying current of thought, represented by the various cults and creeds, which is common and universal, which one and all may, with immense profit, follow. This common and universal ideal of happiness has not been pourtrayed so beautifully and graphically in the theological and philosophical literature of any other country as in that of India. The Aryan Rishis paid more attention to spirit than to flesh. They did not seek so much for material prosperity as they did for the culture of spirituality. They did not care so much for this world as they did for the next. They sacrificed earthly comforts at the altar of spiritual well-being. They thought out the great problem of human existence in all its minutest details, and the solution, they have vouchsafed to humanity, is truly worthy of their spiritual insight and culture. This grand solution of the grand problem is couched in words, which for their literary excellence and high spiritual tone, will steer clear of the Scyllas and Charybdis of agnosticism and free-thinking materialism, and contribute, ever and anon to the solace of suffering humanity. "Whatever object is beloved unto men leads to their misery; a person knowing this attains to everlasting happiness." These golden words occur in the Ninth Chapter of the Eleventh Book of the great work *Srimad-Bhagavatam.* And they serve as a beacon light to erring mortals. The Rishi, in a solemn voice, asks every body to shun what is dear unto him, if he wishes to enjoy everlasting happiness. It is the attachment to what we love that begets misery in this world. True happiness lies in sacrificing what we hold dear, true happiness consists in sacrificing our own selves for others. And this spirit of self-sacrifice, this spirit of sacrificing what we hold dear—is the true ideal which the Rishi has beautifully described by saying—"The ospreys that are not fleshy slay one that is fleshy, and the latter, forsaking its flesh, attains to happiness." This grandest conception of *sattwa-guna* or the quality of goodness is hardly to be met with in any other literary work. A person becomes a divinity on this earth when he is entirely pervaded by the quality of goodness. Influenced by *rajas* or the quality of passion (*i.e.*, the self-centering tendency), the osprey kills the fleshy one, which, influenced by the self-sacrificing tendency, attains to happiness by giving up its flesh. Thus the person, who is capable of sacrificing his own self, who is capable of rending asunder all the fetters of attachment, can roam at large, shorn of anxieties, and declare with the Rishi, "I have neither honor nor dishonor; I have no thought of a house-holder or of those having children; sporting with, and being attached to, my Self, like a child I rove. The foolish child, who can set forth no endeavour, and he who has gone to the other end of qualities, both, freed from anxieties, are, ever and anon, filled with great delight."

Thus we see that the conquest of desires and worldly attachments, is what leads to the acquisition of true happiness. What is worldly, what partakes of flesh, what is tinged with earthly attachments, what draws us near and nearer to what we love in this world, cannot bring on true happiness. This has been nicely described in the episode of Pingalá, a courtesan, who understanding the true nature of happiness, renounces the world, once for all. The story of her life is full of lofty ideals, and may always be read with profit, and I make no apology, therefore, to quote it here *in extenso* from my English Translation of the *Srimad Bhagavatam.*

" O prince, formerly there lived in the city of Videha a courtesan by the name of Pingalá; hearken, I have learnt something from her. One day wishing to take her lover to an appointed place, she, well-dressed, stood at the out-gate at the proper hour. O foremost of men, beholding persons passing by the roadway, she, hankering after riches, took them for men who would be able to give her handsome money. They (all) having gone away, she, living by hints, thought :—'Some other rich man might turn up who would give me profuse money.' Having her sleep thus stolen by false hopes she stood at the gate and while thus going in and coming out, the dead of night set in. By this expectation of money her mouth was dried up and heart rendered poorly. She then acquired great disgust (for the world) engendered by thought, but leading to happiness. Hearken, I shall relate duly what was said by her with a disgusted mind. Disgust for the world is like a sword for the noose-like hope of a man. O child, one, who has not acquired disgust for the world, cannot snap the fetters of the world.

PINGALA said :—Alas! how senseless and of what uncontrolled mind am I; behold the extent of my foolishness. Vicious as I am, I have expected the fulfilment of my desire from an impious master. Forsaking the adoration of the Eternal and Real, Who always lives near and gives satisfaction and wealth, ignorant as I am, I have sought a trifling person, who cannot satisfy desire and who gives only grief, fear, sorrow and affliction. Uselessly have I afflicted my soul by the cursed life of a public woman; I expected wealth and satisfaction from a lustful, vicious and lamentable person, though my body was bought by him. What female, save myself, seeks the house filled with urine and excreta, the bamboo pillars and inmates whereof have been created by bones, which is covered with skin, hairs, and nails and the nine doors whereof are giving out (refuse). Forsooth, I alone am foolish in this city of Videha, for, disregarding Achyuta Who confers self-gratification, I have sought satisfaction from elsewhere. He is the friend, the most beloved lord and soul of all beings; purchasing Him with my own self I shall sport with Him like Lakshmi. To what extent have men, subject to birth and death and conferring objects of desire, and the celestials subject to Time, brought about the satisfaction of their wives? Forsooth, by some action, the Divine Vishnu has been propitiated with me, since this disgust for the world, leading to happiness, has sprung in me, who am filled with wrong hopes. Had I been unfortunate, I would not have met with miseries, the source of this disgust for the world, by which a person, snapping all fetters, attains to happiness. Placing on my head the benefit rendered by Him and forsaking the wrong hopes created by vice, I shall seek refuge with the Lord. Revering with contentment what I shall get and maintaining myself therewith, I shall enjoy with the *átman*. My soul has been drowned in the well of worldliness; the worldly objects have pilfered its vision and the serpent of Time has devoured it; who else but the Lord can save it? When you shall see the world devoured by the serpent of Time, and in consequence thereof you shall be disassociated with the unreal objects of this world, you shall then be able to save your own self."

THE BRAHMANA said:—Having thus determined, Pingalâ gave up all hopes of securing men, and, resorting to peace, she quietly went to bed. Hope is the great misery, and the absence of it is the greatest bliss, and by cutting off the hope of getting a lover, did Pingalâ obtain a sound sleep."

## CHAPTER XVII.

### THE NECESSITY OF UPASANA.

UPASANA is the *sine qua non* of spiritual culture. Without it no one can attain to emancipation. It is a necessity, which an individual soul feels in its attempt to be at one with the Absolute or Supreme Soul. But this worship, true and divine, does not consist in external rituals and ceremonials, but in meditation of the nature and being of the Supreme Spirit. A religious aspirant should always worship the Ever-Existent, All-Intelligent and Ever-Blissful Supreme Brahman. He should never abstain from worshipping his God, however circumstanced he may be in the world.

Now admitting the necessity of meditation for a religious aspirant, the question arises regarding the period of meditation. Should a man meditate all through his life, or stop at a certain time? This question has been answered most satisfactorily and in unmistakeable terms in the sacred writings of the Hindus. It is recorded in the *Vedánta Sára* :*

"Whether one should practise *Upásaná* as long as he likes or till his death? One should practise meditation as long as he likes till he acquires mental concentration. A man, even after death, is associated with the mental attitude which he experiences on the eve of death. Therefore one should practise meditation till his death."

Expounding *Upásaná*, the author of the said excellent work says:—"*Meditation* to be *en rapport* with the tri-attributive *brahman*

---

* उपास्तीनां यावदिच्छमावृत्तिः स्यादुतामृति ।
उपास्त्यर्थाभिनिर्वृत्तेर्यावदिच्छं मतूर्पार ॥
अन्त्यप्रत्ययतो जन्मभाव्यतस्तत्प्रसिद्धये ।
आमृत्यावर्त्तनं न्याय्यं सदा तद्भाव वाक्यतः ॥

4—1—8 (Adhi).

by concentrating the mind, as the system of *Sándilya* cited in the *Chhandogya Upanishad.**"

Meditation enables the individual to concentrate his mind. As in the *S'ruti* "By the study of the Védás, by sacrifices, and by meditation, Brahmanas seek to know Him," and in the *Smriti*† "Refraining the mind (the eleventh organ) and the rest of the ten organs from innate passions which each of them is subject to, extinguishes sin." And as a result of this intense meditation the individual attains to a high state of spiritual existence.

This meditation or mental adoration of the Deity cannot be carried on spasmodically. By

---

* उपासनानि सगुणब्रह्मविषयक मानसव्यापार-
रूपाणि शाण्डिल्य विद्यादिनि । ६ ।

*Vide* Dr. DHOLE's Translation.

† What was delivered by human authors, law, traditional law, the body of memorial law (civil or religious).

practising meditation once or twice a day, and being engaged otherwise the rest of the day, one cannot attain to emancipation. For this, one must practise meditation always and be continually in a prayerful mood of mind. Emancipation, or freedom from the ills of existence, is not such a cheap commodity that one can acquire it for the mere seeking for it. A man must have his mind entirely concentrated in the Supreme Self; and it is only then, when this state of absolute mental concentration is realized, that it is possible to acquire emancipation.

The period of this spiritual discipline, and exercise of mental concentration extends over one's own life-time. It is said in the *S'ruti* :* —"One should worship the Self till he acquires emancipation." Even a person, liber-

---

* What is heard or revealed. Name for Védás and Upanishads.

सर्वदैवमुपासीत यावद्विमुक्तिः ।

ated in this life, *i.e*, one who has mastered his own self in this world and has disassociated himself from earthly associations, should worship it. It is thus said again in the *S'ruti** :—" Even persons, liberated in this life, worship the self."

The nature and character of this meditation or worship has also been described in the scriptures of the Hindus. It is said in the *Vedánta Sutras†* :—Not by ordinary *Upásaná* nor by meditation that one can acquire *mukti* or emancipation, for this sort of meditation does not either beget the true knowledge of *Brahman* or secure the region of Brahma. As a simple stroke does not pierce the vitals and, therefore, cannot bring on death but a hard stroke does the same, so emancipation is

---

* मुक्ता अपि ह्येनमुपासते ।

† न सामान्यादप्युपलब्धेर्मृत्युवन्नहि लोकापत्तिः ।

secured by deep meditation and not by simple and easy *Upâsanâ.*

The posture of *Upâsanâ* has also been described in our scriptural works. It is said in the *Vedânta Sutras.**

One should worship on being seated. For, if a man lies down at the time of worship he may fall asleep, or if he stands up there may be agitations of the mind which are all very strong impediments in the way of true worship.

It is elsewhere said in the same sacred book†:—"One should worship the Deity by meditation." It is also recorded there‡:—"One should not move at the time of worship."

Even in the *Smriti* it is said, that one

---

* आसीनः सम्भवात् ।

† ध्यानाच्च ।

‡ अचलत्वं चापेक्ष्य ।

should sit down at the time of worship. It is recorded in the *Vedānta Sāra* :—*

"At the time of lying down, rising up, and going, one's mind is agitated. Therefore for concentrating the mind, one should take his seat.

There is no restriction about the time and place regarding the worship of *Brahman* ?

"One should worship wherever his mind becomes fixed and concentrated."

It is again said in the *Vedānta Sāra* :‡

"One should worship wherever his mind becomes fixed." Thus we see that concentration of mind is the most essential element of religious meditation. There is no necessity

---

* शयनोत्थानगमनैर्विक्षेपस्यानिवारणात् ।
धीसमाधानहेतुत्वात् परिक्षिप्यत चासनं ॥

† यत्रैकाग्रता तत्राविशेषात् ।

*Vedanta Sutra.*

‡ चित्तस्यैकाग्रसम्पादके देशे उपासीत ।

of a particular place or regulation. The injunctions of the *Vedânta Sâra* are very clear on the point. There it is said* :—

In the worship of the Great *Brahman* only the purity of mind is essential. Bathing, fasting, lamps, incense, flowers and other external objects are absolutely unnecessary. These external paraphernalia of religious worship have, however, some value to a novice who has not yet been able to control his mind. But to one who has got above this incipient stage of spiritual culture, they are absolutely of no use. To him mental concentration is the one thing needful. The Lord Shiva thus explains the subject to Pârvati :—

" One can worship the Great *Brahman* as he likes either by words, or by his body, or by his mind, but his mind should always be pure. Whether bathed or unbathed, whether fed or

---

* एकाग्रस्याविशेषेण दिगादिर्न नियम्यते ।